ADVANCE PRAISE FOR

New Possibilities for Early Childhood Education

"Susan Bernheimer offers teacher educators an important call to action with this significant book. Not only are the students' stories compelling, but the idea of using these stories to reshape our emphasis is something we must take very seriously. In the tradition of Myles Horton and Paulo Freire, Bernheimer reminds us that teachers are students and students are teachers. Even though I have taught early childhood students for over twenty years, this book gave me a new perspective and a challenge I plan to undertake. I encourage all who care about cultivating new leadership and expanding the voices and perspectives in the early childhood field to make this book a focus of serious consideration."

Margie Carter, Adjunct Faculty, Pacific Oaks College and Shoreline Community College, Seattle, Washington; Author, Training Teachers: A Harvest of Theory and Practice

"In *New Possibilities for Early Childhood Education*, Susan Bernheimer shares a creative, insightful way to present early childhood education to a class of nontraditional students from impoverished backgrounds. She successfully blends student interviews and vignettes into the more standard instructional material and involves students in active participation. Bernheimer challenges us to revisit our teaching practices and invites us to test the use of the life stories of our students to enrich our curriculum."

Docia Zavitkovsky, Past Present, National Association for the Education of Young Children; Author, Listen to the Children

"Classrooms are sites of struggle where narratives collide and subjectivities are made and re-made in the image of both the limitations and possibilities for transformation. Susan Bernheimer's book visits the charged arena of the college classroom where she encounters the moving testimonials of nontraditional students. She engages their stories and their lives with sensitivity and insight. This important new book documents a journey of hope and a pedagogy of possibility."

Peter McLaren, Professor of Education, Graduate School of Education and Information Studies, U.C.L.A.; Author, Che Guevara, Paulo Freire, and the Pedagogy of Revolution

"Many childcare providers in the United States are poor women whose own childhoods were often cut short by the demands of poverty and other hardships. Those that enroll in college-level early childhood preparation programs hear the formulas for 'normal' development and the preferred child rearing patterns of middle-class, white America, a culture far removed from their own experience. Susan Bernheimer and her participants treat this dilemma in a most compelling manner. Their stories add significant insights into childhood and human development that can enrich our theories and practice of early childhood, our curricula, and our preparation of early childhood educators. Bernheimer's sensitive ear and her participants' willingness to share their stories provide us with a new possibility for transforming early childhood education to include childhoods that are disadvantaged as well as those that are privileged. Once you begin to read these stories and Bernheimer's analyses, you will never again view early childhood education in the same way."

Mary Poplin, Dean of the School of Education,
Claremont Graduate University, California

"New Possibilities for Early Childhood Education is a valuable tool in the work of creating effective, equitable adult learning environments. By providing the opportunity for her adult students to give voice to their life stories and by weaving these stories into early childhood education courses, Susan Bernheimer truly honored her students' identities, experiences, and knowledge, giving us the opportunity to extend our horizons and knowledge. By recognizing the impact of gender, class, and culture in the lives of adult students, Bernheimer also takes us to the universal core of education that liberates and deepens all of our humanity. I urge all adult educators to make *New Possibilities for Early Childhood Education* part of their working library."

Louise Derman-Sparks, Faculty, Human Development, Pacific Oaks College,
Pasadena, California; Co-Director, Early Childhood Equity Alliance;
Author, Anti Bias Curriculum: Tools for Empowering Young Children

New Possibilities
for Early
Childhood Education

Rethinking Childhood

Joe L. Kincheloe and Janice A. Jipson
General Editors

Vol. 23

PETER LANG
New York • Washington, D.C./Baltimore • Bern
Frankfurt am Main • Berlin • Brussels • Vienna • Oxford

SUSAN BERNHEIMER

New Possibilities for Early Childhood Education

Stories from Our Nontraditional Students

PETER LANG
New York • Washington, D.C./Baltimore • Bern
Frankfurt am Main • Berlin • Brussels • Vienna • Oxford

Library of Congress Cataloging-in-Publication Data

Bernheimer, Susan.
New possibilities for early childhood education:
stories from Our nontraditional students / Susan Bernheimer.
p. cm. — (Rethinking childhood; vol. 23)
Includes bibliographical references (p.) and index.
1. Early childhood teachers—Training of—United States—Case studies.
2. Women teachers—Training of—United States—Case studies. 3. Minority
teachers—Training of—United States—Case studies. 4. Minority women—
United States—Social conditions—Case studies. I. Title. II. Series.
LB1775.6 .B47   372'.071'5—dc21   00-067535
ISBN 978-0-8204-5296-8
ISSN 1086-7155

Die Deutsche Bibliothek-CIP-Einheitsaufnahme

Bernheimer, Susan:
New possibilities for early childhood education:
stories from our nontraditional students / Susan Bernheimer.
–New York; Washington, D.C./Baltimore; Bern;
Frankfurt am Main; Berlin; Brussels; Vienna; Oxford: Lang.
(Rethinking childhood; Vol. 23)
ISBN 978-0-8204-5296-8

Cover design by Lisa Barfield
Cover art by Nicole Pollard

The paper in this book meets the guidelines for permanence and durability
of the Committee on Production Guidelines for Book Longevity
of the Council of Library Resources.

© 2003, 2004, 2006, 2008 Peter Lang Publishing, Inc., New York
29 Broadway, New York, NY 10006
www.peterlang.com

Printed in the United States of America

Table of Contents

Foreword

Susan Bernheimer has written a book that is informative and brave. She willingly reveals how unprepared she was to work with the nontraditional students in her classes:

I had always thought that, as a college instructor, I would have all the answers. I thought it was my job to walk into the classroom, give a fascinating lecture, apply this information through group activities, and occasionally lead a stimulating discussion.

In a profession in which knowledge and expertise give status, the author admits her helplessness as she floundered for answers. Susan tells of coming face-to-face with students who could not immediately respond to this environment. They were silent and occasionally hostile.

She reveals the struggle as she deconstructed her shift from practice to praxis, warts and all. The textbooks were filled with layers of complex educational theory and images of comfortable middle-class families. Starkly absent was the reality of lives crippled by poverty. When Susan discovered how anonymous her students' lives had become, she knew that she must bring the stories of her students into the classroom. And what powerful stories they are.

The women interviewed spoke with poignancy and honesty. They were desperate to be released from the poverty that defined their lives. They wanted to become teachers and to save other children from an all-too-familiar world of neglect, abuse, ill health, and hopelessness. This book shows how the stories supplemented the textbook and bridged the classroom gap for these nontraditional students. They acknowledged the wisdom and courage of their life experience.

With minimal guidance and counseling from the community college system, our nontraditional students are attempting to engage. They lack the resources that many middle-class students take for granted. They must somehow survive on inadequate finances. Often they are the sole provider and guardian for their children. Some are still struggling with English as their new language. Most depend on public transportation, which is slow and inefficient.

What is special about this book is that Susan takes us through her own process as well as that of her students. Consequently, this book chronicles growth that truly extends both ways from teacher to student and from student to teacher. Together they created a learning community in which everyone was valued and where everyone's voice deserved to be heard, and needed to be heard if everyone was to learn.

I hope that you share in the power and poignancy of the voices in this book. I also hope that you are able to be as honest and open in analyzing your behavior with and toward the students in your classes as Susan has been in this book.

Renatta Cooper
Director, Jones Prescott Institute, Hixon Center for Early Childhood
Pacific Oaks College
Commissioner, First Five L. A.

Acknowledgments

The writing of this book was a journey I could not have taken alone. The words on every page speak of courageous human lives that dared to cross the borders of their known world in search of a larger dream. To those women who graciously shared their lives with me in the hope of helping others, I dedicate this book.

A looming question haunted my life for many months: "How can I write a book that truly captures the truth, spirit, and wisdom embodied in the women's stories?" The answer came through the loving guidance, understanding, and extraordinary skill of my editor and friend, Anne Wood. I am indebted to her partnership.

I would like to thank the faculty at Claremont Graduate University for their support in conducting the research that formed the basis of this book. Lourdes Arguelles, Alfred Louch, Philip Dreyer, and Michele Foster led me into new ways of thinking and writing. I especially want to thank Mary Poplin, who never wavered from her vision of the important message of the women's stories.

This book stands upon the shoulders of other early childhood educators. Elizabeth Jones, Louise Derman-Sparks, and Janet Gonzalez-Mena, in their search for understanding and respect across cultures, led the way down this road less traveled. I appreciate Renatta Cooper's recognition of the book's importance in bringing new voices into our field as she sat reading rough drafts of this emerging book. I am particularly thankful to be a part of Pacific Oaks College and its continuing mission to further social justice in our world.

I thank Docia Zavitkovsky and Annabelle Godwin for their inspiration and support over the years. I am profoundly grateful to Janice Silver, Gwen Dophna, Emma Steiner, Linda Cole, and Mark Gunderson for their diligent work in opening the doors of higher education for all students, regardless of their economic, social, racial, or cultural background.

Beneath my solitary work of writing was an interconnected world of encouragement and help. My deepest appreciation goes to Fran Schireson, who quietly and with devoted care spent many laborious hours transcribing the women's stories and providing technical editing.

I am grateful to friends who loyally stood by me with never-ending encouragement. I especially want to thank Vivian Rothstein, Jennifer Glaser, Marsha Epstein, Eve Triffo, and Sharon Rogers for giving their time to provide feedback for my writing. I thank Stephanie Pollard and Nicole Pollard for graciously extending their artistic talents in designing a cover for this book.

My father, Leonard Schireson, enthusiastically supported my continuing education, letting me know that a woman can be appreciated as a well-educated person. And my mother, Bea Wartell, was my first role model of a woman who grew up in poverty and learned to live with grace in two worlds. I thank my sister Judy and my brother Ben for their support and encouragement. My greatest teachers have been my two children, David and Adina, who have taught me the real meaning of unconditional love.

To those who are taking the time to read and ponder the stories and ideas in this book, I extend my sincere gratitude. I can be reached at sbernheimer@pacificoaks.edu or my website: susanbernheimer.com.

Introduction

This book is about the hidden gifts of the stranger's story. They are stories that teach us of struggle, strength, hope, and courage. Starkly missing from the standard textbooks and films in early childhood education, they are the stories of the most vulnerable of the nontraditional students who step into our college classrooms and too often find a frightening and alien world.

Sixteen Latina and African-American women living in poverty shared their life stories that form the basis of this book. Although the names have been changed, the words are theirs. The women tell of real and courageous lives we could not know from outer appearances. They represent the unspoken voice of our increasing numbers of nontraditional students: the frightened homemaker reentering college, the uprooted immigrant, the divorced mother, the unemployed factory worker—all taking fledgling steps into a new world.

Although the women interviewed for this book are not typical of the entire nontraditional population, they offer new perspectives needed to support the courageous choices of all our nontraditional students. The increasing diversity in population demographics along with shifting economic, social, and political dynamics around the world is demanding that our field become more inclusive. The women's stories cast light into hidden struggles and triumphs that often take place beyond the boundaries of our academic research. Their stories open the door to a new level of understanding needed to meet the challenges facing our field today.

These women all attended community college teacher preparation programs. Yet, they remained largely unnoticed or were seen simply as misfits. They did not look, act, speak, or dress like traditional college students who typically fill our campuses. On the surface, nothing in their lives had prepared them to step into this fearful place, the college classroom. As they faced vast new challenges, there was little in their new surroundings that provided the needed support and guidance. Inadequate orientation and limited assistance in academic counseling added to their fears. Difficulty with basic skills and limited familiarity with the language compounded their difficulties.

My goal as a college instructor was to create a dynamic and meaningful educational environment for our future teachers. I wanted to make sure the students learned the information, completed their assignments, and passed the tests. Like other instructors in our field, I wanted to keep alive their excitement about working with young children.

The struggles that many of my students faced were evident from the beginning. Something was always missing in my work with them, and I began to feel as helpless as they did. Eventually I was able to search for answers. These answers did not come from academic literature. They came from the women themselves.

Their stories told of staggering hardships; they also told of the many unrecognized gifts these students can bring into our programs. These are students who struggle as bicultural women living on the edge of mainstream society. They know the many subtle ways that poverty, ghetto neighborhoods, or life in a new country can affect the lives of both children and parents. They are the ones who can best understand children facing a multitude of challenges in our society today. They offer the life experience that no textbook or curriculum can replicate. They teach us of new possibilities for preparing teachers around the world.

Shabatay (1991)[1] believes that classroom settings are places where people come together as strangers. People with vastly varying backgrounds and a common goal carve out their futures and learn together. Whether our classrooms are made up of students living in another country or from differing ethnic and cultural backgrounds within our nation, it is stories that allow us to break through barriers and honor the richness of diversity.

This book is an acknowledgment of the courage that these women have demonstrated by choosing to use their lives to help our next generation of children. Their stories chart new and more viable possibilities for all of us. To the many college instructors who tirelessly work in the privacy of their classrooms, my hope is that these stories and insights will affirm the importance of your dedication and assist your efforts in preparing teachers for tomorrow's classroom.

NOTE

1   Shabatay, Virginia. "Stranger's Story: Who Calls and Who Answers?" In *Stories Lives Tell: Narrative and Dialogue In Education,* edited by Carol Witherell and Nel Noddings. New York: Teachers College Press, 1991, 136–52. Shabatay explores the role of the stranger in our society and how stories can be used in our classrooms to bring strangers together.

Chapter 1

Our Journey Begins

The phone was ringing persistently as I walked through the office for instructors at a Los Angeles community college. The head of the Early Childhood department called over to me, "Can you add another course to your teaching schedule?" As a part-time instructor I was always looking for additional classes. She handed me the phone. The voice on the other end told me they needed an instructor for a class in child and adolescent development. The class would consist entirely of women on welfare. The caller reassured me that these women tested high enough scholastically for college-level coursework. Would I do it?

I was pleased with the chance to teach another course but immediately found myself faced with a more daunting task than I ever could have imagined. These women, I soon discovered, faced a multitude of challenges. Academic struggle was only one. They were strangers in a strange land. Their foreign jewelry and used clothing spoke of other places, hidden difficulties, and standards of living far removed from our middle-class academic institution. Displaced and frightened, they sat with their thick textbooks in front of them, anxiously waiting for information from another world.

I watched their faces lose all animation as they listened to my attempts to explain abstract concepts. Each class became another struggle to get the women to understand and remember technical terms and theories. Yet, we needed to move quickly if we were to cover the broad range of age groups and multiple aspects of development. Among the many topics addressed were physical development such as the function of myelin sheaths, saltatory growth, the cephalocaudal principle, and various other dimensions of growth. Additional subjects included Piaget's theory of cognitive development from substages of representational thought to concrete and formal operations, gender identity, Erikson's psychosocial stages of development, and Kohlberg's theory of moral reasoning (Kaplin, 2000). [1] The amount of material that needed to be covered left me feeling doomed to failure with this group.

I watched the students sink into feelings of inadequacy and shame with each new bombardment of information. I persevered, hoping that I could find ways to make the material meaningful and real to these women. Occasionally, films, along with observations and group projects, provided excitement and discovery. But overwhelmingly, these class sessions were marked by discouragement and disconnection.

In desperation, I started skipping over intricate scientific descriptions and giving simple definitions to inflated concepts. I began looking to my students for guidance and new answers. I knew that behind the silence, this group of women had genuine concerns and insights to express. I started searching for ways to bring their lives into our classroom learning.

I did not realize I was beginning a path that would lead me further and further away from standard teaching practices and into serious questioning of our teacher preparation programs. Just as the women in this book were headed into unexpected and vast life changes when they entered the college classroom, I was starting my own journey into an unknown world. This book tells of these two simultaneous stories. The first is about a particular group of nontraditional students who attended early childhood teacher preparation programs in the Los Angeles community college district. The second tells of my personal experience as an instructor in these programs. Our journeys would come together in powerful ways, catapulting us into surprising connections and changing our lives forever.

While struggling through this class, I received a call from another community college program serving students on welfare. They needed someone to teach the same child development class for the upcoming semester. Reflecting upon my current challenges, I knew these students would need a class that could introduce them to the field in a way that would include their own life experience. I offered to create an intro-ductory class that would teach basic concepts in early childhood education without using a textbook. The department accepted my proposal but only as a noncredit class.

Excited about this new course, I looked forward to my next teaching assignment. Following the directions given me, I got off the freeway at an exit near downtown Los Angeles. A left turn would take me into the heart of the financial district with its towering buildings, hotels, and upscale restaurants. I made a right turn instead and found myself driving down dark streets with dilapidated buildings and bus stops full of waiting people. Carefully tracking the designated streets, I soon arrived at a community college serving some of the poorest students in Los Angeles.

The parking lot was located in the basement of the building. I climbed up two flights of littered stairways into the main part of campus. The jacaranda trees in full bloom, a still-vibrant reminder of summer, stood in stark contrast to the musky, deteriorating buildings. I walked through the campus, passing groups of African-American and Latino students talking and laughing. Among them were numerous young men in wheelchairs. This was the setting for my introductory class for students on welfare.

Twenty women and two men were waiting for me as I entered the classroom. They were nervous, uncomfortable, and sweating in the scorching room. So was I. Within five minutes, my blouse was sticking to my body. I suggested opening the windows, which did little to cool off the room. They sat staring at me, painfully ill at ease and uncertain about what to do. I stood there looking back at everyone, feeling as out of place as they did. My limited experience teaching women on welfare at another college had not prepared me for this school. We were all facing a new world that none of us felt ready to enter.

I struggled through our first class, often feeling overwhelmed and out of control. The students seemed to be completely unaware of class-room manners. They responded to me by either silently withdrawing or yelling out and interrupting anyone who spoke, including me. The classroom was feeling like a battleground. Trying to keep everyone in order was exhausting, and I seemed to have little impact. Feeling more and more helpless, I was relieved when the session finally ended. Sitting long into the night, I wrote out numerous class preparations that I subsequently tore into shreds. By our next meeting, several students had dropped out of the class. I greeted the news with a mixture of despair and relief.

Often on the verge of tears, I wondered how things could possibly go so badly. I wasn't new to education and considered myself a good teacher. My answer finally came on a particularly desperate day when I turned to them and asked a real question. Not a textbook question. Not a question I knew the answer to, but a real question. "What do you think is most difficult about raising our children today?" They started talking about genuine concerns for their children. I asked another question, "What do you want for your own children?" With sudden clarity I discovered that these students had stories to tell and that these stories needed to be our starting point.

My next assignment asked them to start observing children in their homes and neighborhoods. "What made them feel happy, sad, angry, loving?" Their interest blossomed as they shared story after story. A few weeks later, my initial fear of these students was beginning to leave. We were learning to communicate with each other as we shared our common concerns for children. The class sessions were far from textbook perfect. I felt guilty about those who had dropped out, but small successes were bringing renewed hope.

It was a particularly humid September day in Los Angeles, part of a long string of such days. The assignment had been to watch a group of children playing together in a park, and discussion was in progress. Most class members were participating, some a little more forcefully than I would have liked. While Christina told about her 7-year-old son getting into a fight with three other children, a woman yelled out that it sounded as if it was his own fault. Then another broke in, calling "Hey, why not let her finish?" Christina broke down in tears, sharing how hard it was for her to control her very volatile son. The room suddenly stilled as she stood there crying. It was not a time when I would have cared for my evaluator to step in, but I silently felt grateful that the class had made its first giant step in discussing early childhood in all its complexity.

Looking back on those days of torn-up lesson plans and sleepless nights, I realize I was desperately searching for ways to authentically reach my students. I was slowly moving away from all my usual lesson plans for teaching. I thought about educators as early as the 1950s who had questioned our standard practices in teacher preparation. Arthur Jersild came to the conclusion that "We need to move toward something that is personally significant beyond the façade of facts, subject matter, logic and reason behind which human motives and a person's real struggles and striving are often concealed" (Jersild, 1955, p. 81).[2]

Continuing Lessons

I began feeling more confident in myself as a teacher. It was our fourth week, and students were engaged in a lively discussion. The door suddenly opened with particular force. An angry-looking woman quickly walked into the class. Barely glancing at me, she slammed her books on a front desk and sat down. Shocked, I walked over and said that she must have come into the wrong class. "No, I did not," she responded. Reacting to her hostility, I sharply told her the name of the class. "I know," was her only answer. "You must leave," I insisted. "It's too late to begin the class." "I'm not leaving," she shot back. I looked into her thin, tense face staring at me with open hostility. Who was this wiry, ill-tempered woman wearing an old beige shirt and jeans? Why was she so determined to stay?

The rest of the class had become silent, watching every move we made. I had to show her that I was in charge. "You are not staying in this class," I informed her, trying to keep my own fear and anger under control. "Yes, I am," she snapped back. We defiantly stared at each other while everybody looked on. Finally, she picked her books up and began walking out of the room. When she was halfway to the door, a male student yelled out, "You aren't going to let her make you leave this class, are you?" She whipped around calling out, "No." Desperate now, I still had to find a way to win. "You will not be receiving a certificate for this class," I informed her. This was my introduction to Tanya.

Tanya returned to class the following week. We began the session by sharing the homework assignment. This was a self-reflective exercise on a positive and negative life experience. The students were asked to write how each type of experience taught them important things about living and how this would help make them a better teacher. Person after person began sharing about their lives. Although they included positive times, their real focus was on sharing their most painful experiences. It felt as if the women and men in this class had waited a lifetime for this moment.

The class was becoming a safe place for these students' voices to be heard. It was a place where they could share the truth of their lives. My position as a teacher was shifting as well. Along with the students, I found myself searching for answers to complicated situations. By now I was sure that my clear-cut teaching packages were suddenly obsolete. As a result, our dialogues became more complex each week, bringing new meanings to concepts we thought we had understood.

Tanya also began shifting her attitude as a student. She started writing extensively on her homework assignments. She finished the remainder of the class and then enrolled in another introductory course. Each week she became more expressive and dedicated in her writing. When the course ended, Tanya slipped away quietly, and I would not see her for another year.

When I began teaching a new class in child health and safety, I looked out and saw Tanya sitting in the front row. She smiled at me and I hardly recognized her. She was no longer the defiant, angry-looking person I remembered. She looked open and alert. By our third class, I told the students they would need to have textbooks in order to remain in the course. After class Tanya came over to me. "I'm having trouble getting my financial aid for the book." With desperation she added, "I've tried everything. Talked to everyone I could. They're having trouble getting it approved." We stood looking at each other. "Here," I said, and handed her my book. "Use it until you get the money." I suddenly realized how much we both had changed.

Two weeks later, Tanya came to class with her new book. As she returned my book, she gave me a note. She wrote that the introductory class had changed her life and that I had given her confidence to pursue her dreams and become a teacher. She thanked me for caring about her and said that she would do anything for me, to just ask. Several years later, I decided to accept Tanya's offer. I asked if I could interview her.

A Hard Road to the Classroom

Tanya's life is typical in many ways of the low-income women I would be working with over the next five years. She was raised in South Central Los Angeles. Her mother had nine children. She was the "baby girl" but had three younger brothers. She says of her life growing up, "I've always hurted," and describes the unspoken neglect in her life:

> *I wasn't a child that grew up to be with the fashions. I wasn't into football or cheerleading because my self-esteem wasn't where it was supposed to be at that time. Because I raised my own self. Nobody taught me how to cook. Nobody taught me how to dress. Nobody taught me how to put makeup on or comb my hair. I wasn't taught those things because I wasn't at home you know.*

Tanya quickly moved to the pivotal experience that would change her life forever. "I wasn't a bad child. I was raped at the age of 13." When she told her mother that her stepfather had raped her, the mother refused to believe her. "She didn't believe what I had said. She took me to the police station and left me there. She never believed me." Then I was placed in a detention center. Tanya lived there for seven months before they found her a foster home. She describes her foster home. "The husband tried to rape me. The wife beat me with a stick. I ended up running away from the place. I was still 13." She then lived in a girls' home until she was 18.

Tanya was now 37 years old and a single parent of four children. She had also been helping to raise other people's children, including her nephew, who was a drug baby. Her daughter was 18, her son was 17, and there were two younger children. Tanya told me how well they were doing. "They are not in the streets. They are not on drugs. They don't smoke cigarettes or go to parties." Tanya was a devoted mother who believed that "a child is a gift, not a possession you own."

Because of the pain she had been through in her own life, Tanya talked about wanting to work with children. She said,

> *I kept looking back at the things that went on in my life. Especially with me going through a detention center and going through a foster home. And seeing the different children that were in there. And that made me look back*

and say, "Maybe you can make a little difference in the world," because they
say a lot of kids that are abused they come up to be abusers. And I am one
that can tell them that is a lie.

Tanya was contradicting textbook theory. She went on to say that
memories of abuse can inspire a victim to help other children to escape
such suffering:

That make you care more. Because you were there. And you don't want that
to happen to someone else's child or your own. And I think those type of
people make the best foster parents. They make the best teachers.

I grew up wanting to be a teacher. Once I went through the hardships in
my life, I let it go. But I kept hearing the little theory...the abused will
become abusers. And I became afraid. You know, to be around other
people's kids.

Tanya kept returning to her love of children and desire to be a
teacher and help them. "You want that child to be able to get on TV
and say, "Tanya helped me to get here." She recalled her initial class
with me and how it had rekindled this dream:

It helped me a lot; it helped me a lot. It made me realize that I do have talent
with children. It helped with me being observant. The exercises that we did
for observing—and then it helped me to write down what I was thinking. It
helped me to put myself in the parent's place and also a teacher's place. Not
just a teacher in school but a teacher that can teach other people's children
about life, you know, as they are growing up, and to sit and talk with them.
Because you have a lot of parents that don't talk to their kids.

She became pensive, or maybe she had finished speaking, I wasn't
sure. Then she added with that same conviction: "It made a heck of a
difference. It gives a person their self-esteem back. And that is something that it gave back to me." During her enrollment in that first class
with me, Tanya began teaching children in the Sunday school that her
church offered and decided to pursue a career in early childhood
education.

What Are We Teaching?

Listening to Tanya's story, I remembered my first reaction as she
stormed into our class. How much I wanted to win the battle I set up

between us. I knew my desire to control this woman went beyond one confrontation with a student. I expected to be in charge of the rules, the information, the theories, and the answers that students gave. I embraced order. I followed the textbook and the time-honored teaching methods, but I had neglected the most time-honored method of all: We must start with the student.

I thought of the ways that many of our academic practices diminish students who are not a part of the White middle-class culture. Delpit (1995)[3] found that when significant differences exist between the students' culture and the school's culture, teachers tend to misread students' aptitudes, intentions, and abilities. I recognized how my limited world of White privilege had too easily led me to label students. I hadn't understood my students' style of interaction, and I didn't recognize the expressions of defeat.

I was beginning to question the effects of our incomplete recognition of mental and emotional health in a field based on optimal human development. How could our models be so skewed? Why do so many textbook voices perpetrate stereotyped images of homes in the country or in upper middle-class suburbia and continue to disregard our most deprived students? What if their stories raised new and complicated questions? Is there room in our college classrooms for tragedy and struggle? Do we automatically silence these students by pouring out scientific information in our lectures?

Jo Anne Pagano (1990)[4] believes that all teaching is political, since we situate ourselves in the world through what we know and understand. Our choices about what we teach, how we teach, and how we interpret the texts are ethical choices. I remembered how quickly I wanted to silence Tanya. The theoretical concepts that I brought into working with women in poverty became my own set of prejudices.

I was facing a new set of challenges beyond those of outlining this course. I needed to rethink my use of instructional methods that left little room for the critical element of listening attentively to our students. I would have to scrap the usual ways of working with classroom material, accept that I did not have all the solutions, and welcome a new collaboration. Although I was only beginning a journey toward finding new answers, I knew that our educational design had failed these women. I also knew that this journey would require me to open my heart and hear truths outside the ones I had been taught.

NOTES

1   Kaplin, Paul S. *A Child's Odyssey: Child and Adolescent Development*, 3rd ed. Belmont, CA: Wadsworth/Thomson Learning, 2000.

2   Jersild, Arthur T. *When Teachers Face Themselves*. New York: Teachers College Press, 1955. In the 1950s Jersild became concerned about the way teacher preparation failed to address teachers' self-understanding and the personal meaning of what the students were learning.

3   Delpit, Lisa. *Other People's Children: Cultural Conflict in the Classroom*. New York: The New Press, 1995. Delpit looks at the ways our classrooms silence children in poverty and of color. Her guidelines for inclusivity apply equally well for adults.

4   Pagano, Jo Anne. *Exiles and Communities: Teaching in the Patriarchal Wilderness*. Albany, NY: State University of New York Press, 1990. Pagano believes our educational theories frame how we see the world.

Chapter 2

The Cultural Divide

Bertha held the small coin dangling on a chain as high as she could so everybody could see it. In the middle of the coin was a picture of Jesus Christ. "My best friend gave this to me for protection when I left El Salvador fifteen years ago. I still wear it every day." She carefully put it back around her neck. "This is all I have left from my country. We barely escaped." Bertha sat down quietly, not wanting to go any further with her story. Another day, she might tell us more. I looked at her few reminders of another life, hair wrapped in a twisted bun, small Spanish barrettes, and the necklace she wore around her neck.

This week's class assignment was to bring in a special item from home and write about how it was part of their lives. Memorials from another world were presented: a family picture taken before boarding a boat leaving Vietnam; a small, handmade dress worn as a child in Mexico; an old, yellowing storybook carefully wrapped. Each woman described her precious item and its hidden story. This was a class of immigrant women who had given up more than any one item could show. Their stories told of leaving families, friends, towns, professions, languages, foods, and customs. They told of the many bereavements in their lives as they immigrated to a new country.

Crossing over is a term often used to describe a person's death. It conveys the idea of the soul crossing over from the dying body into a new spiritual dimension. I listened to the women in class that day, thinking of what they had faced in crossing over from a world they knew as home to a strange place they did not understand. I also thought of other women I was teaching in community college programs. Some were immigrants similar to these women; others were born and raised here in poor ghettos of Los Angeles. Yet, they all showed the haunting characteristics of displaced people groping for a way to survive as strangers.

For many nontraditional students, sitting in our classrooms means crossing from a world they understood (even if it is painful) to another world they do not know. It is a world their lives have not prepared them for; it requires new skills amid a place filled with unfamiliar sights, sounds, and customs. For these students, stepping into this unfamiliar world takes an ongoing act of courage.

The risks facing our nontraditional students, particularly those from oppressed groups, are greater than they could have realized upon entering our programs. In addition to the alienation of being a stranger in this new world, they also risk losing the worth and identity of their lives. As they read our theories, statistics, and predictions, they will hear societal judgments against those living marginal lives. The real stories of their lives will never be seen or understood in the textbooks they read and the films they watch in class. The heroic nature of their journeys to our classrooms will disappear within a masculine-based, middle-class mode of learning and interacting.

Falling without Stop

As a former student, Diane met with me to talk about her life. We sat together outside the confines of a classroom structure. Beginning with great caution, she unfolded a story that we do not hear in our standard teachings. Diane was 41 years old. She is an African-American woman who grew up in South Central Los Angeles with her mother, father, and two sisters. She enjoyed her childhood and always wanted to be a teacher. The only troubling memory of her community was the increasing violence in the neighborhood. Her mother began making sure that she and her sisters stayed inside most of the time when they were not in school. Her childhood would give few clues that she would end up crossing from a place of living dreams to one of hopeless despair. It is an important story, one that is common to single mothers today living in poor ghettos.

Following graduation from high school, Diane got married. After eight years her life shifted radically when her husband left her and their two children without any further contact or financial support. She describes this time:

> *I have worked all my life, but then when my divorce—my marriage ended, I was at that time forced to be on welfare because I had two small children and I didn't really have enough skills to actually be a teacher. But I didn't give up; I kept on going to school. And I stayed with my mom and my father for about four or five years. And then I eventually found a job working in a childcare center.*

Diane eventually had a third child but did not remarry. She continued working hard to support her children and taking courses in child development. She was barely earning enough to pay rent and buy food for her family. In 1992, Diane began her downhill slide into severe poverty and despair. The first cracks in her uncertain foundation started to appear:

> *So I was teaching in the school in '92. We was already getting up maybe like five o'clock in the morning to be to work by eight o'clock because I was taking the bus at that time, me and my daughter. And she was attending the same school I was teaching at. And we were still running late every morning. So that got me in trouble. And the director said, "Well maybe you could get up earlier." And I say, "Well, buses don't even run before five o'clock in the morning."*

During that year, she became ill with diabetes and high blood pressure, causing a series of shattering effects on the delicate stability of her world. Diane's condition continued to deteriorate and with increasing repercussions. She explained, "I started feeling anxiety, like…I'm failing as a teacher, as a person. And so eventually, I had to give up that job because I really started getting sick. I lost a lot of weight. I went down to about 70 pounds." Becoming unable to care for herself, she had to take her children out of school to help her. She finally got the diabetes under control and decided to open a home daycare business. She describes what happened:

> *And that is when I started my family daycare. That was successful for a year. And it probably would have lasted longer than that...but the environment we were in wasn't the type of environment where I wanted children to be. Well, we were in an apartment, a very large complex. It had to be close to 80-some units. And at the time, I had noticed a lot of people that were dealing with drugs and that were doing it inside the apartments. And then I noticed how the ladies were dressing. It was just unbecoming. And I just didn't feel like okay. And I felt like I am losing my daughter, you know! And I knew that she was growing up, but I felt it was too fast.*

Realizing the dangers of the environment in which she lived, Diane gave up home daycare and took two jobs to provide for herself and her children. She describes how her children reacted to her working every day and evening. Her "son went into a shell," and her daughter was "just the opposite. She became more outgoing. And more loose. Running with wrong crowds and things. So I was losing my children." At this point, Diane remarked to her mother, "I don't know which is the worst, to be able to financially care for your children and not be there for them. Or be there for them and not be able to take care of them financially."

Still continuing her search for a way to support her children and spend time with them, Diane moved to San Bernardino looking for cheap housing and a job. Unable to find work there, she brought her children back to Los Angeles:

> *So that is when I came back to Los Angeles County; I went for a period of time without any money, any food, anything. So we were living in a shelter but all this occurred during that time frame when I had my nervous breakdown. That was the second shelter that we had been in, and we had been in about two hotels before that, because we couldn't afford the rent.*

Welfare reform had reduced her payment for food to $160 per month for four people. At this point, Diane went to a doctor asking for some counseling, "because a lot of people just end their lives." No help came out of the visit. Diane lost all hope of finding any solution to her problems. Blaming herself for this hopeless situation, she fell into a state of mental despair:

> *Because it was just more than I could bear. It was too many things happening at one time, and I couldn't cope. So it was a very high level of stress. I said, "I can't take care of my kids. I can't keep my marriage. I can't keep a job." I mean there were so many things. I just didn't think I was worth anything, you know. And so they put me in the hospital for a while because I would...just scream out uncontrollably to where my kids would have to call the paramedics. And it had gotten so bad that I didn't even know I was doing it. I was just sitting there. And they said I was just sitting there, crying. And screaming at the top of my lungs.*

Beyond Individual Failure

Diane's story is more than a personal struggle of a low-income mother. It reflects the increasing poverty and deterioration of family stability in the African-American community since the 1970s. By 1990, two-thirds of all Black children were born to unmarried mothers. The majority of Black women today live as single parents as a result of economic hardship, unemployment of men, and sex-ratio imbalance in the community. Diane is part of a community dealing with the repercussions of long-term discrimination and oppression. This hopelessness has taken on many forms, such as the AIDS epidemic, drug use, and the high incarceration rate of parents (McAdoo, 1998).[1]

Diane's unbearable suffering did not only come from the terrible difficulties she faced as a single parent living in poverty. Her greatest pain came from the increasing realization that she lived in a society that did not care as she watched herself and her children fall into hopeless despair. Adding to this pain were her unrealistic expectations of herself and the accompanying feelings of shame and self-blame.

Diane's tendency to blame herself was the result of continuing poverty and discrimination. Left to bear extraordinary burdens, African-American women have created an image of the strong matriarch who acknowledges no personal pain, can bear all burdens, and will take care of everyone (Greene, 1994).[2] Diane's feelings accurately mirrored our society's perception of those living marginal lives as incompetent and lazy people who are ungrateful for the gestures of support offered by mainstream society (Freire, 1997).[3]

Through Diane's faith in God and the support of her church, she eventually gained the strength to return to college and her studies in early childhood education. She continued battling her physical condition of diabetes and the stress of living in poverty:

> *And I have to admit it. At times, it is very difficult to keep a high self-esteem.*
> *It's difficult to concentrate on what I need to do—like going to school or*
> *whatever. Because, I have to admit, there are times when I am depressed and*
> *I want to give up. Sometimes we don't have enough food, or I can't pay the*
> *rent. So it's difficult.*

Listening to Diane's harrowing slide into financial, physical, and emotional ruin, I marveled at her strength in returning to college. Similar to other low-income women, Diane sees college as a last hope for a meaningful profession and improving her life. What is the message she will receive in our classrooms?

Our Classroom Message
I thought of Diane sitting in classes week after week learning to care for other people's children while her own life as a parent and her children's lives were silently falling apart. I thought about the underlying message given to her during this time about the role of education: It did not include what she most needed; it did not include a caring community of people sharing experiences as part of their learning and growth.

Parker Palmer (1993)[4] believes that our classrooms teach more than a body of knowledge or a set of skills. We actually teach a way of being in the world. Our current mode of teaching, designed to create a neutral learning environment, keeps our focus on external information. This approach to education teaches an undeclared curriculum that outer knowledge is important while the world of our student's inner self is of little use in the educational process. By centering our education only on external data, we may be sacrificing some of the most critical aspects of learning. We are denying our students the benefits of their personal experiences. Our classrooms are not teaching students ways to listen, ways to share, and ways to truly hear and value others and themselves.

While these students study scientific theories of child development, their own lives remain anonymous. Our focus on external information keeps the suffering and painful emotions of our students far away from the academic setting. Diane and others like her struggle to memorize abstract concepts, beliefs, and theories that have little relation to their own lives. Our "banking system" of education based on depositing information into our students teaches a powerful message: Leave your real lives outside the classroom. You have nothing to contribute. We will give you the right answers (Freire, 1997).[5]

Diane's story reflects common conditions women in poverty bring into our classrooms. Such stories tell the real and complex issues facing women as they struggle against overwhelming odds. They offer glimpses into a complicated world our field needs to better understand. These human stories take students out of the emotional disconnection of standard academic learning into the warmth of our shared humanity. They teach students like Diane and every person in the class that they are not alone in their struggles.

As an instructor, I wondered about the cost to our students as well as our field when such disturbing and important stories are kept out of our classrooms. Without these stories, we are preventing our classrooms from becoming living models of the caring and compassionate community we want these future teachers to bring to other children and their parents. And we are continuing to hide the true conditions these women live with in our society.

Diane's story tells us about the personal anguish behind a mother struggling with the ravages of poverty. It is a story of increasing desperation as she encountered the ongoing harsh and unsupportive conditions in her life. It is a story that is currently being lived every day by millions of mothers in poverty. And it is a story that could never be understood through statistics or textbook descriptions.

The Hidden World of Poverty

The hidden quality of those living in poverty extends beyond the classroom. Poverty in American society is invisible to our mainstream culture. We have designed freeways, housing projects, and businesses so that it is easy to avoid direct contact with such communities. Existing in their own separate world, the nation's poor can easily be ignored except for occasional statistics or newsbytes.

The invisibility of poverty masks important questions reflecting a culture's values. We avoid the critical questions, such as "Who are the poorest people in our society?" In 1998 nearly one in every five children, 13.5 million, lived in poverty in the United States. Along with their children, single mothers form the largest group living in poverty.

Racial inequality continues, with Black and Hispanic children having more than twice the poverty rate of White children (Children's Defense Fund, 2000).[6]

Although economic growth has brought about a slight decrease in the number of poor children over the last few years, the actual conditions of poverty are worsening. The income in the average poor family with children was less than $9,000 per year in 1998. Over 5 million American children live in families earning as little as $6,502 a year. Sadly, 74% of poor children live in families where someone worked outside the home but earned wages too low to lift them out of poverty. (Children's Defense Fund, 2000).

Early childhood education must understand poverty and its effects in order to serve these families. The low-income women in our teacher preparation programs understand firsthand how poverty permeates their existence. They know how it weaves its way into every dimension of life. It silently permeates each waking hour and follows its victims into their sleep. It determines their identity: the food they eat, the places they live, childhood, motherhood, job opportunities, schools, speech, clothing, transportation, future goals, and a basic sense of one's meaning in the world.

The multifaceted repercussions of poverty are often obscure to an outside observer. Low-income parents feel more economic pressure, argue more about money, have strained parent-child relations, and suffer from physical ailments and unhealthy housing. Almost three out of four poor families with children cannot afford their rent or mortgage and utility payments based on federal guidelines. They often live in crowded, roach-infested, and moldy living quarters with structural and plumbing problems. They are eight times more likely than the nonpoor to be without a car. And they are more likely to have no telephone or bank account. Marriages in poverty break up at twice the rate of non-poor families (Children's Defense Fund, 1998).[7]

Blaming Single Mothers in Poverty
The vast majority of my students in community college early childhood classes were Latina and African-American single mothers trying to beat the odds against themselves and their children. These women all lived with a burden few people talk about: the devastating perception of our

culture that single mothers in poverty are to blame for the suffering and difficulties they face every day.

This belief covers up the true causes of poverty, those that lie in structural inequalities of access and opportunity. It places responsibility on the most vulnerable citizens, poor single mothers and their children (Polakow, 1993).[8] This denial of poverty's true causes is reinforced in our classrooms as these women listen in shame and silence to unforgiving statistics and theories.

Latina and African-American mothers in this country are particularly likely to be poor. Yet, we know little about their experiences of poverty and motherhood, which may be different from those of Caucasian women (Belle, 1990).[9] Similar to African-American women, immigrant women live within highly complex social dynamics that are largely misunderstood. In our colleges they face the challenges of a transitional generation crossing lines of country and gender. The stories of the Latina mothers in this book illuminate how these dynamics can unfold with unexpected repercussions.

Crossing Lines of Country and Gender

Every Thursday morning I drove over to the Head Start building near downtown Los Angeles. By 8:30 A.M. I was walking into the classroom cautiously balancing my coffee, donuts, and books. I sat at a table along one side of the room, carefully laying out my morning meal. The plain, square room became colorful and lively as the women arrived from different parts of the city. They were all taking advantage of receiving one year of child development classes offered to mothers interested in teaching. The class would begin at 9:00 A.M.

As the weeks passed, we developed an unspoken routine during this borderline time together. While I settled down and arranged my food, the women would glance over, smile briefly, and keep an eye on me as they engaged in animated conversations. Most of their conversations were in Spanish. Many of the women were immigrants from various Latin American countries. As soon as they saw that I was comfortable, they began coming over singly or in pairs to chat with me.

At first our chats seemed like a trivial passing of time before class started. I learned of their everyday concerns and the struggles and intricacies of living as immigrant women moving beyond their established roles. These chats became a doorway of greater understanding and trust between the women and me.

It was during this casual time before class that Olivia arrived one morning looking highly distraught. Quickly walking over to me, she pleaded, "I have to talk to you. Not here. Someplace where we can be alone." She looked pale and frightened. I quickly found a hidden staircase behind the classroom and quietly sat with her while she cried. Finally, between sobs, she began telling me what happened. "My husband left me and our three children last weekend. He said he didn't love me anymore and has another girlfriend. I don't understand why he left. We were a perfect family. I did everything I could to be a good wife and mother." She described her physical symptoms of shock: "I can't eat or sleep. The doctor said my pulse and heart rate are getting dangerous. I don't know what to do. I waited all week to talk to you. You're the only one I trust."

I listened as Olivia described her world falling apart. She looked at me, desperately searching for answers. Watching her grief and confusion, I thought about the dangerous risks these women were taking in attending classes. Not only were they first-generation college students, but they were also threatening the basis of their Latino social structure. I was not surprised to hear what happened to Olivia. I had watched her blossom from a frightened, insecure woman with difficulties in English to a successful student. A month earlier, she had been selected to attend a Head Start conference and was thrilled. Now she was facing the loss of her family.

Olivia's story tells of common issues facing women and girls from a Latino background who have immigrated to the United States. The importance of the family is a characteristic of the Latino culture, yet the immigrant experience and poverty strain the family (Espin, 1997).[10] Immigration sets in motion forces that can draw women away from the inner world of the families. These changes threaten gender roles and the designated responsibility of women as the guardians of culture and family traditions. When immigrant women develop new independence or social status, tensions and a disruption of the husband/wife relationship often occur (Suarez-Orozco and Suarez-Orozco 2001).[11]

Olivia began her life far from the classroom she was now sitting in. She was born into a family with ten children, living in severe poverty on a farm in Mexico. Yet, even in spite of limited finances and strict female gender roles, Olivia showed determination and strength in her fight for an education:

> *I remember they didn't have no money. You know, to send me to school. And I told my mom, "Mom, I would like to study something." And she said, "I feel real bad, but we have no money." I feel bad because my dad doesn't want to spend the money on me. He was very angry. "What will you study? You are a woman. You are going to get married. Why are you doing that?"*

Olivia's mother agreed to secretly help her get money. She and her mother made dinners to sell so she could attend high school. Even though she sacrificed food in order to attend high school, Olivia was happy with her decision:

> *When I was studying in my high school over there in Mexico, I remember they didn't have no money. And during that time, she only bought me a pair of shoes a year. Only three dresses. Wash and dry and wash and dry. But you know I got no money. I don't care. I want to study. And I used to not eat over there at school, because I never had money in my pocket. And I was like a toothpick. 'Cause all my friends, they used to have money. And they used to tell me, "You not going to buy anything?" And I said, "No, I'm not hungry." And you know what? I was starving!*

After high school, Olivia came to the United States to escape the poverty and moved in with her sister. She met a man through her church and they married. Following an expected path, she soon had three children. It was while she and her son were attending a Head Start program that Olivia decided to accept its offer of free college courses in child development. She was unaware that this decision would take her outside the agreed-upon structure of her culture and marriage.

Olivia was unexpectedly facing the effects of powerful and contradictory social forces that commonly take place in immigrant families. Transitions are always stressful. Olivia was now encountering transitions on multiple levels, including educational status, cultural changes, family structure, financial loss, and emotional upheaval. These changes would be part of even more complex challenges that Olivia will face as a single parent with children who were also straddling two cultures (Suarez-Orozco and Suarez-Orozco, 2001).

Unforeseen Decisions as an Instructor

While listening to Olivia's story that morning, I had to face new issues as an instructor. Our respective roles left room only for a caring response to her crisis, encouragement to stay in school, and suggested referrals. Yet, I also knew that an expanded perception of my role was taking me into gray areas where I was asking new questions. Should I shift topics for that day and include issues of divorce? Should I share with her my own personal experience of going through a divorce with young children when I returned to college for a master's degree? I began reappraising our divided roles as Olivia sat before me in despair. In the immediacy of that moment, I was caught off guard. I realized with new intensity the full reality of Noddings's assertion that the dynamic of caring that exits between the teacher and student is the essential ingredient of education (Noddings, 1984).[12]

Looking at her eye-to-eye, I shared with her how I had also been through a similar painful experience many years ago. Letting her know that I had no idea of the outcome between her and her husband, I was certain that she would be fine no matter what happened. Looking at me with amazement, Olivia stopped crying. "You? You have been through something like this? But you are happy! You are wonderful! I can't believe it!" I watched hope come into her face for the first time. This hope increased as we discussed issues of separation and divorce in class, including ways to support children during this time. Olivia later shared about what she learned that day:

> I was crying the whole class. But I came to my house, and I was thinking about my kids. So I made a schedule. We started new routines. And I started thinking that even if I am alone, a single mother, I have to do the best I can for the children. I started taking my kids to the library. To the park. We started making things at the house like cookies. So, I learned a lot.

Olivia was choosing to continue her new path. Her faith was helping her maintain strength as she struggled through a lonely and difficult course:

> And God gave me the opportunity to study as a teacher. ...And you know, I studied child development. And when I got those classes,...I went through the separation from my husband and it was very painful for me. 'Cause you know, ...when my husband was with me, we were a happy family. My children and I never thought it would happen to me because we were very

close to each other. And well, it happens. It happens. But I never stopped studying. I kept studying. And you know what? God helps me. Makes me to study. And it was very painful for us. But God gave me the opportunity to study and to be independent. 'Cause I was very dependent on him. I couldn't do anything by myself.

This will be a path that requires her to continue crossing boundaries into unknown territory as she journeys further away from the world she knew before making the choice to return to school.

Conclusion

Listening to these women's stories, my own world as an instructor turned upside down. I never understood the full reality behind immigrants coming to the United States until Bertha and Olivia shared their stories. I never realized the dangers these women faced in choosing to return to school. I could not have known the vicious, downward spiral of single mothers in poverty before I heard Diane share her own experience. Most of all, I never had to see the limitations of my own beliefs until I stepped outside my prescribed role and modes of teaching.

Is it possible that we cannot see the extraordinary gifts sitting directly before us? I think of Bertha, Diane, and Olivia sitting in my classes. Without their stories they appeared to be insecure students, struggling to read our textbooks, understand lectures, complete assignments, and pass the tests. It was easy to view them as "difficult" students and a burden to higher education. It seemed logical to ask the question, "Why bother?" It was so easy to misjudge them.

Stepping beyond my traditional role opened a barrage of new questions about early childhood teacher preparation. Our programs are meant to educate students to work with families of diverse cultural and socioeconomic backgrounds. How can we possibly exclude the stories of the very women who have lived these diverse experiences? How accurate are our guidelines and knowledge base for teachers if we exclude the stories of those people most silenced and oppressed in our society? What unexamined assumptions have led to such gaps in the content and pedagogy of our field?

Women such as Bertha, Diane, and Olivia are needed in our classrooms as leaders showing the way to others who are faltering on the rocky, uncharted path of first-generation college students. These are the women who can stand on the shoulders of their past and reach out with understanding and experience to help children, parents, and other students who feel alone in our world. They will be the role models that parents turn to and the advocates for children who need them. It will be through their stories that our field can expand in new ways to become truly vital and effective. The stories that follow can open the doors we have long needed to walk through to a bigger and more inclusive world.

NOTES

1   McAdoo, H. "African-American Families: Strengths and Realities." In *Resiliency in African-American Families,* edited by H. McCubbin, E. Thompson, A. Thompson, and J. Futrell, 17–30. Thousand Oaks, CA: Sage Publications, Inc., 1998.

2   Greene, B. "African-American Women." In *Women of Color: Integrating Ethnic and Gender Identities in Psychotherapy,* edited by L. Comas-Diaz and B. Greene, 10–29. New York: The Guilford Press, 1994.

3   Freire, Paulo. *Pedagogy of the Oppressed.* New York: The Continuum Publishing Co., 1997. From his work in Brazil with people in poverty, Freire formulated a philosophy and tools for educating people to move from a place of silence to critical reflection and dialogue.

4   Palmer, Parker J. *To Know as We Are Known.* New York: Harper-Collins Publishers, 1993. Palmer proposes ways to create a classroom as a community of learners seeking truth together.

5   Freire, Paulo. *Pedagogy of the Oppressed.* New York: The Continuum Publishing Co., 1997.

6   Children's Defense Fund. *The State of America's Children.* Washington, DC: Children's Defense Fund, 2000.

7   Children's Defense Fund. *Poverty Matters: The Cost of Child Poverty in America.* Washington, DC: Children's Defense Fund, 1998.

8   Polakow, Valerie. *Lives on the Edge: Single Mothers and Their Children in the Other America.* Chicago: The University of Chicago Press, 1993.

9   Belle, Deborah. "Poverty and Women's Mental Health." *American Psychologist* 45, no. 3 (1990): 385–89.

10 Espin, Olivia M. *Latina Realities: Essays on Healing, Migration, and Sexuality.* Boulder, CO: Westview Press, 1997.

11 Suarez-Orozco, Carola, and Marcelo M. Suarez-Orozco. *Children of Immigration.* Cambridge, MA: Harvard University Press, 2001. The authors present a comprehensive and updated picture of the dynamics of immigration taking place and how these forces affect families and children.

12   Noddings, Nel. *Caring: A Feminine Approach to Ethics and Moral Education.*
     Berkeley, CA. University of California Press, 1984. Noddings provides a
     philosophical and practical view of classroom practices based on a responsive and
     caring relationship with students.

Chapter 3

Emerging Stories

The car quickly swerved, missing mine by several inches. Honking his horn and angrily waving his arms, the driver sped away. With sweaty hands I grabbed the steering wheel tighter. "Pay attention!" I screamed at myself. This was the third time I almost hit someone. I just wanted to get home. I needed someplace where I could think in privacy. After having finished another interview, I felt overwhelmed with emotion and confused about many beliefs that I had never before questioned. I did not expect this level of emotional shock.

Planning my interviews carefully, I felt prepared for anything. I barked orders at myself for days before each one. "Bring extra batteries, phone numbers, recorders. Call the woman and remind her. Be clear about where and when." What I could not have planned for was hearing the truth of these women's lives.

With each interview, disturbing and nagging questions grew in their intensity. How could I be so shocked about my students' life stories? I had chosen this field to better understand and support people's lives. Becoming an instructor in teacher preparation programs became my focus. I was motivated by the belief that our students were the key to fulfilling the promise of this work. Yet, the women I had just interviewed had been students of mine. And neither our classroom experience nor our textbooks had prepared me to truly know and support them.

All the women openly stated that they were studying early childhood education because they recognized the unique contributions that they could offer. They expressed a passionate commitment to make a difference in a world wracked by pain and suffering. They have lived this pain. They intimately understood it and wanted to help others by using the strength they had gained. In Marcela's words, "I was strong. Because pain make you grow."

Any of these women would have cherished a more comfortable and stable life. Yet, these experiences taught them important lessons about life. They led them to perceive their strengths and weaknesses, to recognize their deepest needs, to become willing to walk the jagged and often risky road toward a new path, and to gain a passionate desire for helping others facing similar types of pain. They led them into their most profound growth and development. Now they wanted to become teachers and bring their hard-earned wisdom to help children and parents.

The women all responded with gratitude and increasing enthusiasm when given the opportunity to talk about their lives. They spoke from their hearts with great passion as they let go of shame and judgment. Again and again, I asked myself, "What silenced these women in our classrooms?" Day after day they sat in classes studying human development. Yet, it was only beyond the confines of our standard academic structure, language, and beliefs that they could unfold the missing stories of their lives.

Telling the Truth
Sharnette sat across the table watching my face carefully as she began talking about her life. Soon she mentioned being in "foster care." I looked at her puzzled. "You were in foster care?" She did not answer but placed her right hand on the table between the two of us. I looked

down at the back of her hand, covered by scar tissue and skin grafts. It lay between us as a symbol of the untold pain in her life:

> *The first time I went was because when I was 4½, my aunt had stuck my right hand into a sink full of hot water and I suffered third-degree burns. And I had to have two skin grafts on my hand. I was 5 years old when I got out of the hospital. And from that point on until I was 18, I was back and forth into foster care. I come from a very abusive family.*

Sharnette was giving me a brief introduction to her life. At 27, she told me of growing up amid the increasing poverty and violence of South Central Los Angeles. Unlike Diane, she would not have the protection of being kept inside and away from danger. Her mother was a single parent of three who was using drugs to cope with her life. I listened to Sharnette's story with both shock and a growing humility in the face of her strength and courage.

The struggles Sharnette faced growing up with poverty, abuse, and rejection did not tell the whole picture of who she would become. She spoke with wisdom, compassion, and commitment that did not coincide with standard theories of human development. According to a large body of research, these painful experiences were supposed to be predictors of a disturbed personality, of a person likely to be abusive to others. This contradiction resurfaced with woman after woman. I finally had to face my own increasing discomfort and sense of growing uncertainty about my long-held beliefs.

A Bigger Picture

The women in this book would agree with modern psychology's emphasis on the value of nurturing in early childhood. It is important for children to be held, read to, talked to, listened to. It is helpful for them to play, listen to music, read books, and hear words that motivate. It is reassuring when the voices and faces in their lives assure them of how important they are. These women whose lives have been so immersed in pain and difficult living conditions had an intense desire to help all children have their needs met.

At the same time, their stories show us the unseen limitations in our theories. They demonstrate how our research does not go far enough and creates distorted beliefs that are far removed from real human lives. Throughout the interviews, they repeatedly recalled the most difficult challenges in their lives and how they led to greater awareness, strength, and wisdom.

Listening to Sharnette's complex inner reflections in the face of adversity, I realized that she was providing some critical missing pieces to our understanding of human development. Sharnette's story unfolded like a strange dance of vivid painful memories interspersed with reflections about the valuable lessons she had learned from her experiences. She was telling a story filled with the intricacies of personal experience, inner reflection, and a remarkable path that would eventually lead to the transformation of her life. Immediately following her description of abuse, Sharnette added,

> But from growing up the way that I did, I've learned important lessons in my life. And I am glad that I did. I've wished for better parents. But the life I've had to live taught me important things about being a child. A child should have the experiences that come with childhood. It is not good to force a child to grow up before his or her time.

At another point in her story, Sharnette shared some of the lessons she learned growing up with a drug-addicted mother:

> *I learned my lesson from watching her. It destroyed her life and caused pain and suffering in me and my siblings' lives. The most important thing that I learned from going through that with her is that a child needs love. No matter what.*

These lessons would eventually give birth to a new vision for Sharnette, one that led her into a life of commitment and service. The path would not be a simple one. By the age of 16, she was no longer living with her mother and was running away from group-care foster homes. Struggling to survive on her own, she began succumbing to her worst fears: drinking, smoking marijuana, skipping school, and living a loose life on the streets.

Sharnette did not know that life on the streets was preparing her for choosing a new path. She was unknowingly bringing herself closer to a turning point that would dramatically shift her life forever. Part of Sharnette's new life would be returning to the classroom of our community colleges with other students just like her. I thought of the loneliness and risk she must face leaving a world she knew how to survive in for another one in which she was a stranger.

Would this be a place where she would be valued for her life of hardship and learning? Would her courage and gifts to our field be strengthened as she faced her fears and inadequacies, learning new skills and modes of functioning? Or would our stereotype of a problematic, poor woman of color be reinforced? Would she sit in our classrooms without a voice, hearing about the need for a perfect middle-class life if one were to become a healthy adult? The women's lives were teaching me another story.

Shame and Silence
I began to observe the dangerous repercussions of our textbook images for women in poverty. Inherently this system suggests that without all the props in place, our children are likely to become flawed adults. According to this approach, the Sharnettes and Ramonas and Marcelas and the entire population that they represent are expected to become burdened and burdensome adults who never recover from their past.

This societal image did not fit the stories I was hearing from these women. Their stories all told of rising above the most hopeless of situations. Their lives contradicted the cause-and-effect picture of developmental theory. Yet, this is the only framework for understanding human behavior they study, and these texts can only foster self-doubt. The women quickly learn to sit silently, yet again, with their growing shame for having lived lives on the edge. There will be no place to share their unique contributions to our field.

This is not a new experience for these women. As social worker Ruth Sidel (1996)[1] found, low-income women of color live in a society that reinforces their negative self-image. The victim becomes victim yet again to stereotypes such as being labeled "lazy" and the "undeserving poor." Our early childhood teacher preparation programs are indirectly continuing to reinforce the women's feelings of inadequacy. Carmen expressed how it feels to be judged as one of these statistics:

I read and spoke with some persons after I had been interviewed with you. And they said for them, it is like a cycle. Like if somebody treated them bad...they felt the same thing with everybody. And especially if they are working with the children, it just kind of a reflection. And to me, I say, "No!" I thinking it is wrong! I think it is the wrong mentality. It is the wrong attitude. Because why would you want to pass on what you went through? You don't want nobody going through that especially if we are working on the children.

I thought of women like Sharnette reading our textbook data. I wondered how they must feel seeing themselves through the framework of theories that offer little hope to those who struggled their way through poverty and isolation. I began to understand the depth of shame these women must feel as they sit in our classrooms and why they take refuge in silence. As Kaufman found, "In the midst of shame, there is an urgent need to escape or hide" (1980, p. 9).[2]

I wanted to find the truth of these women's lives beyond our super-imposed conclusions. This search opened the door to many new levels of understanding beyond my perceptions in the classroom. It began with a more realistic picture of the complex effects of poverty. As an instructor, I could see the outer signs of poverty: the used clothing, missing teeth, poor schooling, diseases, and many losses. I knew the women depended on buses. In class some shared how they had little money for food the last two weeks of every month. But it took longer to discover the true suffering that was taking place beneath the outer appearance. Each woman's story told of costs to the human spirit, of living in despair, of families torn apart, of desperate acts of coping, and of communities with inhuman conditions.

Yet, within their stories of painful experiences, these women were also taking me on a journey into an inner world hidden from our scientific data. Suffering had not broken them or made them abusive. I was learning, instead, about their hard-won resilience and their commitment to serve others. However, I was becoming increasingly alarmed that students such as these were being swallowed up in an underfunded system that had gotten too impersonal and an educational theory that had become too narrow.

The Door to New Possibilities
The women's stories offer us a glimpse into worlds of growth that are not linear; they defy statistics and ask important questions of our field. The women's truths unfolded within the natural flow of simply telling their story as seen through their own eyes and told in their own words. Without a predetermined structure and freed from the distortions of statistics and predictions, their inner truths could emerge. They became the author of their own moral stories by uniting emotion, reflection, and action (Tappan and Brown, 1991).[3]

Their stories provide a key for taking us beyond our current limitations. They could restore a sense of wholeness and dignity to our picture of people's lives. They are stories filled with the intricacies of real life and bring an opportunity for genuine sharing and dialogue in our classrooms. They take us beyond the restricted confines of a banking system of education that immobilizes and fixates people, leaving only adaptation to one viewpoint of the dominant group (Freire, 1997).[4]

Crooked Paths to Wholeness

The journeys that led these students into our field did not follow a straight path. These were paths that twisted through dangerous territory and took many unexpected turns. Most of the women had difficult childhoods that led into increasing dangers during adolescence. Growing up in the midst of poverty left these women entering adolescence within fragile and problematic living structures and with limited avenues available for expressing their emerging womanhood.

An external picture of the women's lives during this time fits common statistical predictions for women growing up in poverty. Over half the women became pregnant between the ages of 14 and 17 years of age. Most went through highly difficult experiences, ranging from leaving their family, dropping out of school, and turning to drugs and gangs. For several women, this life would later extend into more serious problems such as spending time in jail, extensive drug use, and prostitution.

An outside image of their lives would give little indication of the women's eventual path. Yet, an awareness of both their inner reflections and outer actions showed a complex process of growth. The following stories begin teaching us new possibilities of development and paths to wholeness. Our textbooks need to acknowledge these lives that began so precariously on the boundaries.

Irma's Dream of a New Life

Irma's dream was about to come true. At the age of 12, she was finally leaving El Salvador to come live with her mother in the United States. Ten years earlier, Irma's mother had left El Salvador without her four children to find work in Los Angeles. For Irma, this meant being passed around from one relative to another for ten years. By the age of

5, she was finding out the risks of being an unprotected outsider in these families:

> *I was living with my aunt. And we had a cousin. He was older. And he used to, I can't say molested, but you know, touched me. And I just felt weird, 'cause I don't know who to tell. I mean if I told someone, they were going to blame me. So I always kept quiet. So after that, we went to another family. And I don't know. I felt like it was me. Like I had something, I don't know what, but my aunt's husband also tried to touch me. And so I just felt like, "Why they do this? I mean, why? What am I doing wrong?" And I don't know. That's why I felt like that. Get out. So every place I went there was some guy that will try to touch me. I always asked myself, "Why?"*

Although Irma appeared to passively accept this abuse and blame herself, her inner reflections tell another story. Even at 5 years old, she considered reaching out for help and realized it was not available. Irma was receiving clear messages from her aunts that she would receive no protection. In fact, she knew that it would mean putting herself at further risk by being blamed for the abuse. Her aunts, who regarded her as an intruder, were already subjecting Irma to physical abuse:

> *She would ask me to do something in bad ways. Threaten me, "If you don't do it, I am going to kick your behind." Or she would just spank me or hit me with whatever she could find. And I don't know. I just feel like every child needs the parents.*

Irma was looking forward to finally being with her own mother. Arriving in the United States at age 12, she found instead new and unexpected challenges. Irma was shocked and upset to discover that her mother had remarried. Her mother began treating her badly. Irma was put into the public school system without being able to understand or speak English and advanced two grades to match her age. Her mother could not help her because she also barely spoke English.

Irma entered adolescence as a stranger to her home, school, and society. Only her emerging womanhood brought hope of a new life. At 15, Irma fell in love and started to build a new, independent sense of herself. She also became pregnant. Whether consciously planned or not, Irma's pregnancy established a new and independent identity.

Irma's mother was very upset and wanted her to go to a special school for pregnant girls. Irma refused, taking a stand on behalf of her new life with her boyfriend. At 15, Irma was not aware that this life would begin a series of dangerous events, taking her into a world of extreme poverty, abuse, and isolation.

She could no longer stay at home, and her boyfriend only wanted to be with his friends. He put her into a motel where she lived an isolated life with her first baby. At this point, Irma noticed the changes in him:

> *When I had my baby, he started hitting me, abusing me....He gave me a hard time there. He hit me. And once I went to the hospital. And he went to jail. But we went back again. It was just like I couldn't let go. I thought I was at fault when I loved him and so we stayed together. I have four kids now....I was afraid to leave because my mom didn't want me at the house. So I thought, well, what am I going to do? Where was I going to go or what to do with my children? So I had to be there. When I was 24 I had all my children.*

Irma spoke little English and knew of no place to turn for help. Knowing no way out, she tried being compliant with her increasingly abusive boyfriend. But the abuse was becoming more and more dangerous. "I didn't know what was going to happen when he got in. So I was just, I was just scared." By 21, she had three children and lived in fear and isolation. Irma was also heading toward life-changing events. The first incident occurred at age 21:

> *I remember one time that I was doing the laundry. I was doing the laundry and I remember I was cleaning the house. Okay. I had two—I had my daughter and my son. And the laundry was downstairs because I lived in the building. So I went and left the kitchen. I was cooking the chicken, and I left it on the stove and went downstairs to take the clothes out. So about ten minutes later he came back to the house. And all I remember is that he got mad. He said, "Why you not here? Why is the chicken burned?"*

> *So he told me to take the kids to the room. And you know I was afraid of him. So I took the kids to the room. When I closed the door, he grabbed me by my hair. And pulled me all the way to the living room and started hitting me. He broke my nose...he punched me. I mean, he was hitting me! He punched my nose. I started all bleeding. You know, he got scared, because, I mean, it was like a hose, you know, blood all over. So I get scared and I call the police. And he ran away.*

> *Then he called me from a public phone. And says, "You know, Irma, start cleaning the refrigerator and the walls and the floor." Because of the police,*

*you know—"Do you want the police to arrest me?" And I say, "I don't
care." So the police got there and took me to the hospital and gave me a shot,
a tetanus. And so they just did a warrant. So the next time he would— if he
did something to me, they would arrest him. And they did.*

This incident marked the first time Irma reached for outside help,
even against the wishes of her boyfriend. She was beginning to realize
the ultimate danger to herself and her children. Irma was slowly
building up the inner strength and outside resources that it would take
to try and survive as a single parent living in poverty. Three years later,
Irma would make some courageous new choices for herself and her
four children. That's when she enrolled in community college, fearing
the difficulties but hoping to find a supportive environment that would
guide the emerging dream. This step could be her last lifeline.

Lakesha's Dangerous Friends

Lakesha and her three sisters were raised by their grandparents. Her
father had abandoned the family, and her mother had turned to drugs.
Lakesha went through elementary school focused on sports and her
studies. She describes herself as being considered a "nerd" but well
liked. She had a larger purpose in wanting to do well in school. She
wanted to be able to take care of her younger sisters. Lakesha knew the
pain of abandonment. She had only met her father a few times in her
life. She describes an incident that took place as a young girl, while
visiting her mother:

*I can remember being, maybe my seventh or eighth birthday. He called and
he asked me, "It's like your birthday. What do you want? I am going to come
by." And I was like "Wow".... I said, "Daddy, I want this doll." And he says,
"Okay, I'll be there this afternoon"—this was the morning—"to give you
your doll. And we will go somewhere. And I said, "Okay."*

*So it was snowing at the time. And I asked my mom and my great
grandmother to put my clothes on me to go outside and I sat on the porch. I
ate breakfast and I sat on the porch waiting for him. And then he didn't come.
So it was time for lunch. And my mom said, "Well come inside, eat lunch." I
said, "No, my dad is coming. I want to be on the porch. I don't want to
leave." And it was dinnertime. And after dinner, I went right back outside.
Sitting on the porch. And they had to drag me in kicking and screaming later
that evening. And that was the last time I heard from him.*

As she entered adolescence, Lakesha began shifting her focus to friends:

And you know, I think I am the type of person where I let peer pressure get to me sometimes. Because even in high school, if some of the basketball players wanted to cut class....I didn't want to cut. But because I was with them, I felt like I had to cut class.

At the time, I had gotten so out of control that my grandparents were having problems with it. They were always up at the school. It would be...just say it was forty days in one quarter. My teachers would tell them, "Well, Lakesha's been absent twenty-nine days out of my class." And they were shaking me. "What is wrong?" You know, "What is wrong? You've done well up to this point. Why would you want to ruin it now?" and I, my friends were like, "Oh, don't worry about it. We are going to graduate. We will get into college." I wouldn't listen to my grandparents.

Wanting to get back to a productive life, Lakesha decided to make a radical change after graduation. She went into the army for three years. When her grandmother had a stroke, she decided to return home:

I stayed home and I helped my grandparents a lot. I don't know where it happened, but somewhere my life just took a turn for the worst. I was doing things I wasn't supposed to do. I was getting into a lot of trouble. I was young. I was 22 at the time. And I am 30 now. And my grandfather, he sat down with me and we talked. He asked, "Well, why don't you go to school? You are getting into trouble." And I don't know, I just wasn't listening. And this happened for maybe a year.

And I started hanging around with the wrong crowd. It was a crowd that wasn't doing anything for themselves. Just a lot of illegal stuff...selling drugs, being gang-affiliated. I couldn't find myself. I was so confused. I didn't want my friends to think that I didn't want to be around with them or that I thought I was too good to hang around them. So I like fell into it. I don't know if I would have given into peer pressure 'cause I didn't want to do it. But then I felt like if I didn't, then they wouldn't accept me as their friend.

Similar to the other women, Lakesha did not know how dangerous her situation was becoming. Nor was she aware that this very danger would become a turning point for her.

Dimitria's Path to Spiritual Awakening

At the age of 42, Dimitria is a student in child development at a community college. She works in a childcare program and is raising seven children. Although she lives in extreme poverty, her life is one of productive hard work and commitment. She lives a life closely connected to her relationship with God. This would have been difficult to imagine from her life as an adolescent through her mid-30s.

Dimitria remembers her mother struggling to raise six children alone in South Central Los Angeles and never having enough money. She worked during the day and used alcohol to help ease the pain of poverty and ghetto life. Growing up, she was left alone with an older brother who was physically abusive. Her neighborhood church did not provide safety either for Dimitria, since the pastor began sexually abusing her at the age of 8 years.

At 17 years old, Dimitria became pregnant and dropped out of high school. Unable to turn to her family for support, she moved out of the house at 18. Living alone with a baby, Dimitria began looking to a new set of friends. She describes her descent into a life of drugs:

> *And as time went on, I met some friends and I began to smoke marijuana. I didn't really like it, but peer pressure gets you. I wanted to be a part of my friends. They weren't gangbangers, but they seemed like they were always partying. And I started getting into it and finally enjoying it, so I thought. And then I moved on to different drugs and drinking.*

> *And I never forget when I went to visit a friend of mine. I had some cousins that came from out of town. And they wanted to smoke some cocaine. I took them to buy some, and this guy said, "Try this." And it was a pipe. And I hit it once, and I liked it from that day. That was in '81. And I didn't really get into it heavily. Yes, crack cocaine. And I found out where to buy it. How to cook it. How to shake it. And then I sold it. The whole nine yards. And then I became a victim of the drug. And I was no longer able to sell it. I became a user.*

Dimitria describes what happened to her during the time leading up to her turning-point experience:

> *I lost my children. During this time, in 1991, I have seven children. I have five girls and two boys. I lost my children to my mom. My mom got custody. And my sister-in-law got custody. They took the children. And two of my children went to their father. It didn't stop me. It was like a relief of my*

responsibility. I know in my heart I love my kids. And I had to live within myself. But I couldn't find nothing. I'd say it was a relief, because they were being taken care of. My life had become real dysfunctional. I was raped during this time. I had my money taken before. Even going to jail. And that was really devastating when the judge said I will have six months. It tore me apart, but after I did the three months. I thought that would be a turnaround. But it didn't. It took two more months.

Dimitria's turnaround tells a profound and difficult story of healing and a growing motivation to serve others. It is the kind of wisdom that emerged from years of risk, challenges, and commitment. It is the kind of story we desperately need to understand in our field today. Yet, she sat silently in my class for many months.

Ramona's Unexpected Discovery

Ramona had grown up in poverty with her parents and five siblings. They lived in a low-income suburb north of Los Angeles. Her childhood also included a volatile alcoholic father. She felt insecure and unpopular in high school. Entering her senior year, Ramona thought she had found the answer to her dreams. She met a handsome athletic boy and fell in love. Ramona became pregnant at 17, and they were married:

When I was 21, I thought, "Oh my gosh! Who did I marry?" because I ended up marrying a drug addict. And I didn't know what to do. So, his drug use continued. I think he stopped when I had my second child. I didn't want a baby anymore. He had promised that he would stop. And then he continued. So I thought I was doomed. And then I got pregnant. I am not happy with the person I'm with, so I kind of didn't want a baby.

At this point, Ramona was desperately unhappy but not ready to take any action. She continued with a detailed account of the events leading up to her turning-point experience:

I remember my mom going with me to the doctor. And I thought "Oh my God! I'm going to have twins." And I thought, "Oh, I'm going to have two more boys," because I already had two boys. So I was just devastated. The worst part was when I was about six and a half months. And again, I looked in my husband's pockets and again I found what I found. And I was devastated and I was so upset. I remember I was throwing up. I was so angry. I was just sick. I was sad about having a baby with this man. And it was terrible. I went into labor.

This was the beginning of a series of events that would bring Ramona to a point of making critical choices she had never considered before. These choices would dramatically change life for her and for her family. The need for societal understanding would be critical.

The stories of Sharnette, Lakesha, Dimitria, Irma, and Ramona resonate for a vast population. Stories of malnutrition, drive-by shootings, violent and premature deaths, desperate longings, and lives stripped of hope. And yet human courage emerges amid the loss. Each woman was headed toward an experience that would crystallize her most painful issue, bringing her face-to-face with the devastation of her current situation. This experience would bring forth a sudden release of inner awareness, eliciting a dramatic shift in her self-identity and the course of her life.

The women's continuing journeys take them from the ashes of a shattered and hopeless world to renewal and an important mission in life. This mission goes beyond personal success and achievement. It is one of offering their hard-earned gifts to children and parents who desperately need this level of understanding and compassion. Preparation for their new calling will bring them into our classrooms and put them at risk in new ways. Whether or not they are able to fulfill this much-needed mission will largely depend on the place we create for our most vulnerable population. We must welcome them into our world of education, and it can only begin with their stories. Their lives need to be a part of our textbook learning.

NOTES

1   Sidel, Ruth. "The Enemy Within: A Commentary on the Demonization of Difference." *American Journal of Orthopsychiatry* 66 no. 4 (1996): 490–95.

2   Kaufman, Gershen. *Shame: The Power of Caring.* Cambridge, MA: Schenkman Publishing Co. Inc., 1980. Kaufman examines the causes, response, and healing of shame.

3   Tappan, Mark B., and Lyn Mikel Brown. "Stories Told and Lessons Learned: Toward a Narrative Approach to Moral Development and Moral Education." In *Stories Lives Tell: Narrative and Dialogue in Education,* edited by Carol Witherell and Nel Noddings. New York: Teachers College Press, 1991.

4   Freire, Paulo. *Pedagogy of the Oppressed.* New York: The Continuum Publishing Co., 1997.

Chapter 4

A New World Is Born

How do you leave the only world you've ever known? How do you let go of a life you know, in spite of its bleakness and failures? All of the women interviewed for this book told of that bold step. The journey did not begin with a neat and tidy plan for the future. It more closely resembled the bloody and painful process of giving birth. For almost every woman the new direction occurred at a tumultuous but defining moment in her life. Although the turning-point experience appeared as one more hopeless event in a progressive downslide, inner strength and personal faith had been preparing them for this moment.

As the interviews continued, I was never prepared for what I would hear. I still felt stunned by each emerging revelation. And yet, sitting across from me was a poised and ambitious woman narrating her story. I began to feel bewildered. "How had these women reached this point in their education?" Their stories were far removed from a path leading to college. They had been trapped, abused, and manipulated in a world that seemed to hold no alternatives. Moving forward with new action meant taking enormous risks with no guarantee of success. It required breaking away from the little support and comfort available in their lives. It meant grasping for an emerging dream. If the dream failed, the losses would be immeasurable.

As educators, it is important to understand this dramatic time, when chaos and poverty reign over new hopes. Through their stories these women expressed the complexities of their attempts at a new beginning. The motivating dream was a fragile one, still under attack by seemingly insurmountable obstacles. But it was a dream born of courage, and it brought them into our classrooms.

Faltering Steps along the Way
Irma spoke quietly into the tape recorder, giving a vivid description of horrific physical abuse from her boyfriend. There was a shift in her tone of voice. Although it would take three more years for a turning-point experience, I recognized signs of her growing strength.

Looking directly at me, Irma began telling about the last incident she encountered with the father of her four children. She had gone out with a friend to run an errand and accidentally locked herself and her four children out of their apartment. When her boyfriend got home and she wasn't there, he locked them out. She waited at a neighbor's with her children, including a 3-month-old baby. By 1:00 A.M., she began a series of actions that would change her life forever. First she called the police and asked for help:

> The police came that night and they were knocking on the door trying to
> make him react. And he said that he would not open it. But the police said,
> "You know, she has the kids, they need milk. They need a place to stay." And
> he didn't care.

The next day, Irma went to the sheriff and had the boyfriend removed from the apartment. This time she was ready to care for her children independently. She found a job and began taking her first faltering steps into freedom. Irma was now willing to face the harsh realities of a single parent living in poverty with four children. Their father refused to work or help financially:

Since then, me and my children—we're going through difficult times. I was working, but my wages were not enough for four children and me. I was paying a babysitter; it was $100 a week. That was cheap. For me it was a lot because I was making what? Two hundred or two-fifty. And it was just for a babysitter and some food and during the week I had to borrow money to go to work on the bus.

But Irma had gained something that gave her new strength. She had a dream for herself and her children. She remembered a kindergarten teacher who understood and cared about her when she felt abandoned by others. Although this experience with a caring teacher was relatively brief, it made an impression on Irma that would become a later source of inspiration for her own work in the world:

I remember when I was in kindergarten. I used to call my teacher Mom sometimes. 'Cause I loved her. You know she was nice. When my brother left me and I would cry, she would hug me. And that made everything fine. You know little things that make you get in touch with— she cared—that's what I think. And that is what kids know and see.

It will help me think about myself and understand the kids, let them know that if they don't have the support at home, they can count with me. I can be there. Like it happened to me. I didn't have the love of my mom or my family, but I had my teacher. So I would like to do the same.

This pivotal memory stood out from her many years of hardship, reminding her of the difference a teacher can make in a child's life. She wanted to become that teacher.

Irma's hopes would send her into our community college class-rooms. She now had new obstacles to overcome. Could she succeed with her unsteady English and no high school diploma? Where would she find the money? Who could take care of her four children? When would she study? Irma revealed the hardships of using food money and taking a loan for college tuition:

Every mommy wants the best for the children. But it is hard, especially for me it is hard because I don't have any family here. Just my kids. There are times that I had to leave them alone to come to school. Because I didn't have the money to pay a babysitter.

Irma's problems were not uncommon. For most of the women, life became far more difficult after their decision to create a different way of living. They were not only facing new and often overwhelming challenges for their futures but had to confront the repercussions of their past experiences.

A Moment of Awakening

Similar to Irma, Dimitria went through a dramatic shift in the midst of a particularly painful period in her life. Unfortunately, she was additionally burdened with legal repercussions. After spending time in jail for using drugs, Dimitria hoped she would be able to change the direction of her life. There was no immediate change. Two months later, however, she would go through an experience that changed her life forever:

> And one day, I just had a spiritual awakening. I was walking through this alley, and I had drugs and alcohol. I just felt like I had everything on me, and I was drinking. And I stopped under this tree to get high. Everybody used to meet out there to get high. But there was nobody back there when I went. Normally there was ten to fifteen people just getting high. But there was no one there except me.

> I sat down and I went to get high. And I couldn't get high. And I began to cry. I began to ask God to forgive me. And give me my life. I wanted my children back. It was like I saw a vision of me living different, and I just began to cry and pray. And I said, "God help me, I am tired of this." And I went into a drug program May 16, 1993. And it was like a strange place. You know. Just really strange and beautiful. There was a change in my life.

Dimitria described the aftermath of this unexpected spiritual awakening that led her into leaving a life of drugs and alcohol. She became part of a support program but still lived with the ghosts of her past as she struggled toward a new dream for her future:

> Once I got clean, I feared everything around me. I felt guilty. I felt responsible for everything my children had been through. I held myself responsible to come to this decision that it was over. Now drugs and alcohol was over with. I wanted to live...I couldn't hold on to old ideas and try and get a new person. I had to come up with some new ideas, some positive ideas—some motivation ideas. Some things I would like to have in life. I just didn't know how to put them together. And I began to pray.

In addition to odds that already seemed impossible, women such as Dimitria and Lakesha had to confront the lifelong burden of time served in jail. Lakesha was arrested and convicted of being in an automobile with friends who had an unregistered gun. Ironically, this became the event that turned her life around and brought her back to school. She shared the difficulty of her return to the classroom:

You know, so I said I might as well use it and start doing something positive. So I just let that whole crowd go. Not easy at all. It wasn't easy, the first year or so. The first couple of semesters I was here, it was pretty hard.

Lakesha successfully followed through with her new commitment, working two jobs and getting on the dean's list for academic excellence. But her credibility continued to be suspect because of her arrest and conviction:

That one year, I was affiliated with the wrong crowd. It really hurt me. And it is like something that is going to follow me, you know, for the rest of my life. And it is something that if I want to get another job I have to go through explaining again.

The history of our world is a continuing testament to the strength and resiliency of the human spirit. As I recorded the stories of these women, I often felt that I was witnessing the triumph of human courage amid terrifying adversity. They were rising from the ashes of a shattered life to become future teachers who would, in turn, lead other troubled children to find their way to a happier life.

Healing and Contribution
The women's common desire to become teachers was matched by a desire to become healers. They did not want to run away from the nightmares that had almost destroyed their lives. Instead, they wanted to gather strength and embrace the lessons. Women like Lakesha, Dimitria, Sharnette, and Irma all knew how it felt to be trapped in a bleak world with seemingly no release. They knew what it was like to be judged as a failure, to feel hopeless and alone. But they had also experienced, however briefly, how it felt to have somebody who understood and who did not judge them. They now wanted to use the

strength, compassion, and understanding they had gained to help others.

Sharnette recalled both the hardships of her childhood and her first meeting with the woman who would change her life. Living on the streets at age 16, Sharnette was taken to meet Alicia, a foster parent for teenagers. Sensing this woman could be trusted, Sharnette took the risk of going to live with her:

> *She was nice. She didn't talk mean. She talked to us like we were humans. She talked to us like we mattered. We were not little scraps of trash on the ground. She cared extremely well. No matter what kind of problem you were having or how many difficulties you were having, you could go to her.*

This was the caring environment that brought Sharnette into our community college teacher preparation program:

> *I understand how hard life can be...I can make a difference. And maybe one day make other people make a difference too. I want to be able to help improve a child's life. And that goes for helping a parent, 'cause I know sometimes, with newborns it is difficult. And sometimes what can make a difference with a parent just being angry and tired and frustrated and stressed out is somebody stepping in and saying, "Okay, this is what I am going to do for you; I am going to take your baby for a few hours. You go have mommy time. And leave baby to me." And that can keep a parent from going over the edge. And becoming abusive.*

This wish to use past difficulties to serve others matches the findings of a study done on adults whose lives reflected purpose, fulfillment, and integrity (Daloz et al.1996).[1] A large number of these adults grew up feeling marginal. This marginality contributed to their ability to move between groups, and to recognize more easily "the stranger next door" (p. 73). The personal discrimination that they suffered as young children inspired a commitment to serve others and an awareness of social injustice.

Marcela never forgot the lessons she learned from her own father who abandoned the family. She was giving children the kind of attention that was missing for her when she was growing up:

> *As a teacher, I have given the kids opportunity to express themselves. Because I got beat up for opening up my mouth. I got beat up for saying things I wanted to say. Because my father didn't have the opportunity to*

*listen to my complaints...and because I remember there was a teacher there
to listen to me. And because I remember after parents, the main person is the
teacher. Also, it has helped me to be a better teacher because I understand
the needs of the child. I want to give the children what I didn't have.*

More than half the women interviewed for this book had been
teenage parents. Yet, their children became a critical part of their
motivation to succeed. Rosa, who became pregnant at 14 years old, was
determined to graduate from high school, against the beliefs of
everyone around her. Now at the age of 20, she wants to inspire her 5-
year-old son with the importance of attending college:

*And now that I am coming to college, he knows, "You are going to school."
And that is why I brought him. I brought him last semester, for his birthday.
He came with me to school. And he seen how I come to school. And how I
have to do everything. And he was like, "Gosh, Mom, you do a lot. And I
don't do nothing when I go to school." He thought it was hard. And I told
him, "When you get older, that is what you are going to have to do too."*

From Crime to Prevention
Once the women redirected their lives, all their past experiences could
eventually become a source of strength. In a remarkable paradox,
recovering from a criminal past became a means to saving children in
the classroom. Lakesha discovered that her past experience with gangs
gave her valuable knowledge that could be used to help the children she
worked with as a teacher:

*The teaching has priority. This is what I want to do. Because the children
that I teach, it seems like now children mature a lot faster than when I was
growing up. And so I have some kids in my class that already have some kind
of gang affiliation.*

*I'm so truthful with my kids. And I think that is why we love each other so
much, because I tell them you know, "Well, Miss Lakesha was in a gang. I
wanted to be in gang. I wanted to do this and that." Or when I see students
trying to fight other students, I'm like, "Hey listen, I went through the same
thing." And they couldn't believe it. They could not believe it. "My, Miss
Lakesha! You are our teacher!" And I said, "Well, I wasn't always a
teacher." There is certain things that you have to learn in life before you get
to a point where you can become that teacher. "It is a no-win situation, you
know. You cannot win with gangs at all." And because I was able to relate to
them personally, my personal story, it helped them. And I don't hear it*

anymore. If you mention a gang, "We don't want to be in the gangs. Miss Lakesha told us no! It is bad."

All of the parents said, "Do not leave. You work so well with our children." I think that is one of the reasons why the owner of the school was willing to work with me with the criminal findings because I work so well and because I have so many good reviews coming back to her from the parents at the school.

As a teacher Lakesha gained unexpected allies from her past mistakes. The children and parents she served recognized the importance of her hard-earned wisdom. Both Lakesha and Dimitria knew further challenges lay ahead as a result of their criminal records. But they were also aware that they had gained some uniquely valuable insights needed for our next generation.

New Revelations from Story
One overriding question grew in intensity as I listened to their stories: How can we find a place for these women so that they may build upon their important knowledge and experience? The stories were beginning to provide the answer. Along with gaining a better understanding of their hardships, I was learning of many new sources of strength in their lives. I knew this awareness was critical to getting started.

I had forgotten the role that motivation can play in human life. I had missed the truth behind an outer contradiction. I had not considered a neglectful parent, spousal abuse, gang affiliation, or time spent in jail as the impetus for new dreams that would, in turn, lead to public service. I had never known that one kindergarten teacher could make a difference in a life filled with abuse and rejection. I had never read a theory that discussed the profound life-changing impact of a spiritual awakening. And, I was not aware of the power of a caring foster mother, church membership, or the needs of a younger sibling.

The aftermath of Ramona's story demonstrates the breadth of the new life she embraced. After her turning-point experience, the shock of discovering her husband's continuing use of drugs resulted in the premature birth of their child. Ramona knew how to take action and pursue a better life for herself and her child. She filed for divorce, an event that became a turning-point experience for her husband. The drug use ended, and he became a devoted husband and father. Eight years later, he helps with household chores and the care of their children, while Ramona attends college classes.

Once the women broke away from past structures in their lives, they repeatedly discussed their faith in God as a sustaining force. Alma left her husband who was drinking and becoming more abusive. She took her children and moved in with her mother, who lived in Central Los Angeles. She described being with her 17-year-old son after he was shot by a gang member while talking with his girlfriend in front of their house:

And I saw him lying there. And when I went to him, I noticed how he was face down the way he landed. I went to him and I just turned him over. And I took his pulse. And the pulse was still pulsating, but it was getting weaker. I didn't want him to be facedown. I turned him over and I held on to him. And I just prayed. I prayed. I gave him to God. I had told God, if he has been shot in the head, you gave him to me, you take him. You know he's yours. I was still holding on to hope because I felt a pulse. And then, when I was there with him, I was holding on to him, he was dying. I think he was dying there, slowly.

And I was looking around and when I looked toward the East, there was like a ray. Like a ray of white, real white. Bright-like; starry-like. But I didn't think of anything then until after, way after.

When her son died, Alma had a second spiritual experience:

And that night, I really didn't sleep. Because at that time, my son came to me. And he had the same clothes he had on when he was killed. And he just walked in the doorway. And the door was closed. I had closed the door. But when I sat up and looked, the room was dark. He had come through the door and he says, "Mom, I love you very much. I am just coming to tell you that I am going to be okay." And I screamed, "No, Joey, don't go." And then he turns around and he leaves. And I wanted him to stay there and stay with me and tell me, you know, what happened. I just wanted him to stay a little bit longer.

These two immeasurable dimensions of spiritual connection sustained Alma to continue her journey toward a new life in the face of bottomless grief. It also allowed her to move beyond her initial shock and become involved in groups against gang violence. Although the women ranged in their religious affiliation from no formal religion to active church membership, all their stories included the unconditional support of having faith in God.

Beyond learning about unexpected avenues of support, I was also learning the importance of shared stories as a source of growth, self-acceptance, and renewal. Recovery groups offer indisputable evidence of the saving powers of story. With story comes acceptance. With acceptance come self-worth and new hope.

While our classrooms cannot be viewed as recovery groups, they need to be places where human individuality is valued and where dreams can blossom. For the most vulnerable in that classroom population, feeling accepted is the vital first step. Dimitria recalled her experience with a recovery group:

> When I came in to these doors, they say, "My story is your story." Then I heard people get up to the podium—and this is a meeting where I did not know anyone. And I was sitting there and I cried like a baby because I felt this lady talked about me. Because her life story was the same as mine. And I went, "This lady don't know me, how is she talking about me?" As a matter of fact, we could identify and accept each other for who we were. Or who we are.

It was within this safe environment that Dimitria could listen to the sharing of people's stories and begin letting go of shame. Kaufman (1980)[2] found that when people we deeply value risk their own exposure to become vulnerable and openly acknowledge their imperfect humanness we are carried beyond shame.

I began to see how the act of sharing life stories becomes its own path of healing and growth. According to Borden (1992),[3] stories allow people to reorganize experience and reinterpret events. People use narrative stories to change perceptions of life experience, particularly in the face of unexpected or adverse events. Through telling stories, people develop a sense of coherence, continuity, and meaning.

A Prototype for Our Future

As society faces unpredictable social, economic, and political changes, we need new types of strength and insights that are often lacking in standard models of education. According to Lifton (1993),[4] the greatest challenge of our time is developing the skill to live with purpose in the face of upheaval and uncertainty. Inherent in this skill is an ability to fully embrace our lives with all their complexity and contradictions. It necessitates finding ways of expanding beyond the safety of our old beliefs and building our capacity to empathize with others. It is this very process that brings a new population into our college programs.

An important part of Dimitria's healing was listening to stories that included complicated pathways to growth. This recognition helped her acknowledge and validate her own uneven journey, thereby gaining a new perspective of her life. Witherell and Noddings (1991)[5] believe that telling, writing, and listening to life stories allow people to discover their own unique identity and the integrity of the narrator. This realization deepens the understanding of their respective histories and demonstrates their new possibilities. Many of our students can teach us about broader and more realistic ways that people can find support and strength in their lives.

Harrison et al. 1990)[6] found that ethnic minority groups have developed highly complex adaptive methods. Since these groups have often suffered from discrimination, poverty, and racism, they use some common strategies. One of these is the importance of extended families. The extended family acts as a problem-solving and stress-coping system; it provides material support, income, childcare, and household assistance as well as emotional support, counseling, and social regulation.

Another coping strategy is role flexibility within the family. Parenting of young siblings by older siblings, sharing of the breadwinner role among adults, and alternative family arrangements are prevalent in ethnic minority communities (Harrison et al., 1990). Lakesha described how her grandparents and a younger sibling became part of her own turning-point experience:

> Well, after I was in jail, I had to call my grandparents and let them know what happened. And they were like so disappointed. And, of course, my little sister found out. And she was crying. She said, "What are you doing in jail? You are supposed to take care of me. Our grandparents aren't going to be around." She is telling me these types of things I should be telling her. And I just felt like I let the whole family down. And I knew that in order for me to do things so my sister could start looking up to me again, I had to change my life. And I would have to do it fast. And so that is where it happened.

In addition to their supportive dimensions, these coping strategies also create certain obstacles. One prevalent coping mechanism for

African-American families is to teach their children a process of "armoring" themselves in public. In order to protect them from the racism they will live with in our society, children are socialized to maintain a constant vigilance against potential dangers and rejection from others (Greene, 1994).[7] I am reminded of my first encounter with Tanya, and how I reacted to her "armoring" stance by becoming hostile in return. It was through listening to her life story and observations that I was able to break through my own prejudices and coping mechanisms.

For the many women of Latina heritage, a strong emphasis on maintaining the family system can have negative repercussions for those returning to school. Women who choose to focus more attention on their education are often perceived as betraying their family function (Suarez-Orozco and Suarez-Orozco, 2001).[8] Olivia did not realize that her choice to make use of the educational opportunity provided by Head Start was putting her marriage at risk. Adding to her trauma were the extended family's judgments against her for not devoting herself solely to taking care of her home.

Living on the edge, these women are breaking a mold. Unfinished schooling, dire poverty, life on the streets, prison terms, and basic deprivations seem an unlikely partnership with our institutes of higher education. Yet, for those who enroll in early childhood education programs, these experiences form a critical ingredient for understanding generations of young children who enter our schools. The composite hope of these women is that their true potential will be recognized and nurtured as they enter our classrooms.

Pivotal Beginnings

For many, this fragile beginning will be shattered before they can attain their goal. First-generation students have the lowest success rate in obtaining a degree. Fewer than 50% of these students who began college in 1989–90 went on to receive a degree or were still enrolled five years later. Even extenuating factors, such as socioeconomic status, that distinguish them from their peers fail to explain the unusually high dropout rate for first-generation students (National Center for Educational Statistics, 1998).[9]

As first-generation college students, these women are particularly susceptible to feelings of inadequacy as they enter our academic institutions. This is a concern we must pay careful attention to in our programs. Students from similar backgrounds now make up the vast majority of many community college districts, such as Los Angeles. We are what we believe we are, and these students enter our institutions in need of encouragement that will obliterate all the years of obstacles and self-doubt.

For first-generation students entering early childhood programs, our recognition of the immeasurable challenges they face will allow us to find ways of supporting this difficult transition. Many of these students are unknowingly headed for turning-point experiences as they begin to shift their lifestyles to accommodate new priorities. Welcoming them and the valuable lessons they bring will have untold benefits for our field and for their new dreams.

Where Do I Go?

Our educational institutions communicate on many levels just who is welcome, what we stand for, and which priorities we value. Students who "speak well" are more likely to be respected. Those with social poise, confidence, or a traditional high school diploma are more likely to begin with inherent advantages. Those who understand the system are more likely to receive its special services. And those whose voices have been silenced are more likely to remain silent. We are setting up the structure for success and failure. Whether by default or conscious decision, we are passing judgments on our newly arriving students.

Carmen returned to college at the age of 35. Coming to the United States as a young adult, she eventually learned sufficient English and was ready to take the risk of entering college. Similar to the other women, she is a first-generation college student entering a foreign world. Ignorant about our educational system, she describes what she encountered during this critical and frightening beginning:

> *I felt at the beginning like I was lost. I don't know what to study. I don't know where do I have to go?*

> *We have some counselors in here. You need to make an appointment. And then they will give you an interview. And it is a waiting line. You know. They are talking to you, but they are just looking at the long line. And I think, "Why don't they take this more serious?" And at the beginning, I said, "I don't know what to do." And I said I have to design myself. I don't know the language. I have to start learning.*

The lack of concern and availability was felt by other students as well. Alma was born and raised in Los Angeles. She re-entered college in her 40s after studying cosmetology twenty years earlier. Yet, she describes a similar experience as she returned to study early childhood education:

> *Well, when I first came here to college, it was back in the '70s. And I completed cosmetology. But then when I came back in '95, everything was new to me. Now that I'm older, it was my financial thing. But I think the counselors should be friendlier, wanting to help you out. It seems like you go over there, and they just put you wherever. And they put you right into their little program. I don't know why the counselors weren't open that day. They were short-staffed I think. So I didn't get to go that day. And it is kind of a burden. 'Cause you have to go back. And then when you go back, they are not there. They should post signs or something.*

Without a word spoken, the women were already getting a clear message from our colleges. Whether the causes were underfunded departments or information misunderstood by newcomers struggling with language, these students were finding that this new community did not seem to care who they were, whether or not they succeeded, or how they found their way. It gave them their first lesson that they were part of an institution that largely reflects the harsh realities of a society they already knew all too well.

Reality of Student Life

No amount of motivation could have prepared the women for the kinds of personal stress they would face as students. In addition to their daily challenges for survival, they now needed time for attending classes and studying, developing new academic and language skills, adjusting to an aloof academic institution, facing dramatic social changes, and balancing work and family responsibilities along with added financial costs.

A glimpse into the personal lives of the sixteen women I interviewed during a four-month period revealed much that could not be seen in our classrooms: One woman was hospitalized with pneumonia; another was very ill with diabetes; one woman's cousin was murdered; another woman was recovering from her son's recent murder; one woman postponed an interview because of problems with a social worker; and one woman's husband died. All the women were lacking social and economic support systems, so they were going it alone.

Rochelle was living with a man and four children, working at a childcare center, and attending classes at the college. She described her daily schedule:

> My personal life is difficult at home. Dealing with my children sometimes. Not getting enough sleep. Cooking their meals, cleaning them up. Helping with homework. And then turn around and have to do my homework. Where I have to be up all night. And then come here and be exhausted. I thank God that I have transportation. Because some people don't have transportation. And have to get on the bus.

Although Rochelle is keeping up with this demanding schedule, it has affected her emotionally and physically. She was hospitalized for pneumonia during the time of our interviews. According to Belle (1990),[10] low-income women are at high risk of living with chronic life stresses, such as inadequate housing and dangerous neighborhoods. Among unmarried mothers, unemployment, housing problems, and inadequate income were most highly correlated with symptoms of depression.

Yet, this picture does not give the whole story of women who find their way into our classrooms. It does not include powerful forces they set into motion with their decision to transcend personal difficulties. Their stories speak of spirituality, caring people, inner awareness, and coincidental occurrences leading toward their passionate new dream of becoming teachers. Their stories can ignite new passion in the most seasoned teachers or in those teachers who are taking their own first steps.

NOTES

1   Daloz, Laurent A .P., Cheryl H. Keen, James P. Keen, and Sharon D. Parks. *Common Fire: Leading Lives of Commitment in a Complex World.* Boston: Beacon Press, 1996. This is an important study of people living lives of commitment to a common good that embraces diversity, complexity, and the ambiguity of our modern world.

2   Kaufman, Gershen. *Shame: The Power of Caring.* Cambridge, MA: Schenkman Publishing Co. Inc., 1980.

3   Borden, William. "Narrative Perspectives in Psychosocial Intervention Following Adverse Life Events." *Social Work* 37, no. 2 (1992): 135–41.

4   Lifton, Robert J. *Human Resilience in an Age of Fragmentation.* New York: Basic Books, 1993. This book looks at new types of strength and skills that are needed for resiliency in our rapidly changing world.

5   Noddings, Nel. "Stories in Dialogue: Caring and Interpersonal Reasoning." In *Stories Lives Tell: Narrative and Dialogue in Education,* edited by Carol Witherell and Nel Noddings, 157–70. New York: Teachers College Press, 1991.

6   Harrison, Algea O., Melvin N. Wilson, Charles J. Pine, Samuel Q. Chan, and Raymond Buriel. "Family Ecologies of Ethnic Minority Children." *Child Development* 61, no. 2 (1990): 348.

7   Greene, B. "African-American Women." In *Women of Color: Integrating Ethnic and Gender Identities in Psychotherapy,* edited by L. Comas-Diaz and B. Greene, 10–29. New York: The Guilford Press, 1994.

8   Suarez-Orozco, Carola, and Marcelo M. Suarez-Orozco. *Children of Immigration.* Cambridge, MA: Harvard University Press, 2001.

9   National Center for Education Statistics. *First Generation Students: Undergraduates Whose Parents Never Enrolled in Postsecondary Education,* NCES 98–082. Washington, DC, 1998.

10 hooks, bell., *Teaching to Transgress.* New York: Routeledge, 1990.

Chapter 5

The Living Classroom

I watched my new students streaming into the classroom one or two at a time. Few of them looked at me, smiled, or said hello. But they kept coming in, filling up the seats, and spilling into the sides of the room. This was a good sign. I knew that word gets around about classes and teachers. I also knew it would mean turning away many students who would be left with few alternatives at this time.

I was beginning my third semester of teaching Child Health, Safety, and Nutrition at this college, which serves one of the poorest sections of Los Angeles. The student population of the college was almost entirely African-American and Latina. I sat looking around the room as it filled up. A woman in the front row smiled as our eyes met. I nodded and smiled back. I was happy to be here and wanted to use every opportunity to strengthen our fragile connection. Right now, we were all strangers in an old and dreary-looking classroom. We needed to find a connection across the many divides of our lives. I knew the real curriculum of this course depended upon building our own unique community inside this class.

After taking attendance, I announced that each student would be asked to share something about herself, including what brought her to this class. I suggested that people stand if they were willing, so everyone could hear. Embarrassed smirks and nervous discomfort rippled through the room. This was not what they expected. I was already taking away the sense of safety they felt by remaining invisible in the classroom. Several women longingly glanced at the door.

It was going to be a long process of listening to forty-five introductions. I brought up one of my few ground rules for the class. When anyone speaks, we listen quietly, adding that this rule would be important for them to remember when they became teachers. I introduced first with my own story about having two grown children and Jellybean the cat. I told them of my work in the field and how I hoped it would help me to be a better teacher for them. We slowly started our way around the room. Most of the women looked embarrassed, refusing to stand as they introduced themselves. I responded to each person and welcomed her into the class.

Even with the ongoing discomfort, the atmosphere began to change. People were listening to one another and responding more openly as we went along. One woman shared how exhausted she was raising two children, working, going to school, and juggling two boyfriends. Hoots of "I can't handle one" and "You go, girl" were called out as they applauded. We laughed together, and some of the distance began to close. This process was more than our introductions. It was the beginning of making our lives and interactions the basis of learning for this class. It would also be the beginning of moving beyond the constraints of our prescribed curriculum.

Educational philosophy is always a work in progress. I agreed that our textbooks and films contained essential knowledge for working with children. I acknowledged that exams made students accountable for knowing the material. But I also knew students were leaving our programs with large gaps in their learning and in their ability to be effective teachers (Bloom, 1982; Cost, Quality and Child Outcomes Study Team, 1995).[1] For women in poverty and from racial minority and immigrant groups, these gaps inflicted heavy burdens on their personal and educational well-being. There would be no easy answers for sorting through the missing pieces and finding our way this semester.

Undercurrents of Deeper Problems

The problematic nature of our work sometimes leads us to wonder whether solutions can ever be found. Yet, at the most unexpected times, answers can emerge with stunning clarity. One of these pivotal moments took place as twenty of us sat around a large table filled with pastries and coffee. I was attending my first community college faculty advisory meeting. Various leaders from the community had been invited to share their work in early childhood programs with the faculty of this college that served students from a wide range of socioeconomic groups.

Several people made polite comments, describing their role with the agencies and programs with which they were connected. Suddenly, an African-American woman in charge of six Head Start programs spoke with real anger and frustration. "I don't know what you are teaching your students here, but it's not working. They come to teach in our programs and they don't understand the parents or the children. They don't know how to talk with them or understand their problems. Maybe they have a degree from your school, but they aren't doing us any good." Everyone listened, but then we moved on to the next person. The memory of those words and the ensuing lack of response from the faculty haunted me. I knew there was much truth in what the speaker was saying. Over the years, I had seen similar problems.

I remembered walking into the director's office of a childcare center known for its high-quality program serving children from birth to 5 years old. The office was filled with children's pictures, stuffed animals, and comfortable chairs. I was surprised that they needed my assistance as a consultant. The director sat at her desk looking equally perplexed. "You know, I don't understand it. We have good teachers, a warm and caring atmosphere, support for the parents, and a great program for the children. But so many things seem to be going wrong. Staff members argue with each other; parents come in angry from stress; teachers have trouble dealing with out-of-control children; and I get complaints about subs and staff turnover." Summing it up, she added, "I think the teachers just have a hard time dealing with so many people and unexpected things every day. Between crises with children, difficult parents, and getting along with each other, they just can't seem to handle it all."

The next day I visited Margaret, who taught the 4-year-olds. Because she was both a teacher and the assistant director, I felt she could help me gain a good sense of what was happening with the staff. Her room looked interesting, inviting, and safe. I watched the children entering, each greeted with a smile, comments, and some warm hugs. Parents chatted with Margaret and seemed pleased to have their child in her care. She appeared to be skillful in using her education to create a thriving program. I wondered, "What could be going wrong?"

As I spent the day observing the center, the problems became clearer. Before morning playtime ended, a series of unpredictable and emotionally intense encounters took place. An upset girl suddenly bit the boy next to her; a mother broke down sobbing as she tried to leave her infant; a child cut his lip open after a fall; a father yelled at a teacher for releasing his son to a new stepfather the day before; and an argument broke out between two teachers over cleaning up the yard. The teachers often seemed overwhelmed and lacking in the ability to manage these complex relationships.

During the afternoon, Margaret sat with me in the yard. She told me about other complications, such as the parents from India who accused a teacher of "tying up their baby" when they saw it wrapped snuggly in a blanket. Personal animosities between staff members often left everyone tense. A frightened mother kept accusing the teacher of not giving enough attention to her toddler. The difficulties of our rapidly changing society and shifting needs of children and parents were spilling over into this program.

Along with the traditional stresses of childcare programs, the vast changes in living—from financial insecurities, splintered families, pressure to achieve, pervasive presence of media and entertainment, concerns about safety, and our increasingly diverse population—were making new demands of the staff. Fewer and fewer teachers are up to the task.

Further Complications of Poverty
Well-funded, well-respected programs are struggling with societal pressures that did not exist as recently as ten years ago. What about the difficulties facing teachers serving children and parents of racial and

ethnic minorities living in poverty? These children come to school bearing staggering losses. Can their teachers respond to the multitude of crises that occur every day: sudden homelessness, inadequate food, separation from siblings in other countries, the trauma of seeing someone shot, lack of transportation, and alcohol or drug-addicted parents? Can they understand new ways of communicating? More important, can these teachers deal with their own emotions, fears, and prejudices?

The students in early childhood education programs who had the greatest potential to work with these children, because they intimately understood the issues, faced a certain helplessness as they began their work. Rochelle talked about the discrepancy between what she learned in class and what she saw being practiced by well-educated lead teachers:

> Okay, what I was taught and then what I am seeing now, is completely different. You should never shout at children. Never rush them; they go at their own pace. I see a lot of yelling. There is a difference between firm and yelling. And you know, you try and explain to them, "Well, this child did this first." Something that they did not see because they was talking. 'Cause they sit and they talk. They talk, and so they are not really paying attention.

They also noted the discrepancies in our middle-class oriented textbooks. Carmen told how the theories she studied in college did not fit the reality of the children she was teaching:

> I can't say that the theories are really close to the truth. I cannot say they apply, because every child is different. Every human being is different. So, some of them, like the children that really look like the theory, I may say that the theories are really close to them. And to me, those men really study other children.

Yet, the women also expressed appreciation for the information and many new insights they were gaining from their college classes. Insights they would use in their classrooms and in their homes. Marcela shared about using her new awareness of developmental stages with her teenage niece and daughter:

> Stages of development of the child. And the class that impacted me the most is the one that is for the teenagers. Before I couldn't understand why my niece

she acts that way. Now I can understand. And I think I am prepared because I have an 11-year-old daughter. And when she pretends she wants to be an adult, now I understand. And if she asks me if her legs are ugly? I have the answer for her. And if she tells me that she doesn't care about eating much, I know what I can tell her.

Generally, the women expressed a mixture of appreciation and disturbance. As I listened to their many concerns and frustrations, I questioned why were these difficulties so prevalent? Why were these issues never discussed in classes? What was missing in our programs? We need to begin looking for new answers with our most silent students who sit as strangers in our classrooms.

Searching for New Answers

I sat with Olivia for our second interview. She was no longer afraid to express her personal views. She spoke of her most important reason for entering early childhood education. Her response matched those of the other women:

You must love children. If you don't love children, you're in the wrong field. 'Cause how can you be working with childrens if you don't like children? You have to start with your own house. Because this is a hard, hard, very hard field. It looks easy, but it is not. Like I tell you, attitude makes everything. If you are good when the parents come to you and tell you about the problems that they have been going through. And you want to help somebody—I love to do that.

Diane spoke similarly:

Well, number one, I don't know, but the first thing that is coming into my mind is patience. To get anywhere with especially young children, you got to be able to understand that they are children. And having patience and tolerance is a big key in being able to understand the children because children are more active and outgoing than a lot of adults.

Maybe another one would probably be—a lot of people might not say this, but that is what is on my heart, and that is just love and concern. Because, to me, in order to help the person, you have to care about them. You have to want to do it. So when you care about somebody, you want to show them love in return. You know, that is what I reach out to. That is what I reach out to as a teacher. When I am working with children. Number one, I tell myself I am going to take my time and understand this particular individual.

Patience and understanding are discussed in early childhood literature, but they have lost their living presence in so many of our classrooms. Such interpersonal skills cannot be taught as abstract ideas. They must be lived and practiced in our classes. Noddings (1991)[2] writes of her concern that the capacity to respectfully communicate with one another regardless of differences is seriously underdeveloped. It requires placing new value on relationships, dialogue, responsiveness, and flexibility in our approach to instruction. I knew that creating a classroom that modeled this type of caring relationship would mean a radical shift in my priorities and my role as an instructor. I was convinced that this kind of classroom must exist at every educational level.

Bridging the Gap

We were beginning our second week of class. There were schedules to keep, information to teach, assignments and grading to complete. But along with this information, new questions needed to be answered. How can I bridge the gap between their lives and our textbooks? How do I create a safe classroom atmosphere that embodies the characteristics they will need as caring and responsive teachers?

I had always thought that, as a college instructor, I would have all the answers. I thought it was my job to walk into the classroom, give a fascinating lecture, apply this information through group activities, and occasionally lead a stimulating discussion. That suddenly changed as I started to face the real experiences of my students' lives, and a myriad of emotions. Without another approach, my carefully planned curriculum was no longer fitting.

I wanted to keep up the momentum of our original introductions. Students already looked silent and withdrawn again as they entered the room. We began by discussing how important their work will be as teachers. How their own lives give much to build upon. We needed to create a partnership. They were going to be facing a lot of difficult issues with children and parents. Our time together was limited, and we needed to make the most of it. "How many of you have children?" I began. Almost everyone raised her hand. "Have you ever felt scared about leaving them with somebody else?" Hands shot up this time. "How important would it be for you to know your children would be in a safe and healthy place with a loving teacher who understood them?"

Several women called out, "Very important." Looking around at each person, I said, "This is what you are going to be learning in this class."

Our first self-reflection exercise was about to begin. It was a format I would come to use regularly. Everyone took out a piece of paper and began writing about a time they had been left with somebody when they were young. Regarding their health and safety, they were to give one positive and one negative example. "What happened to you?" "How did this affect you?" "What did you learn from this that will help you as a teacher?" They did not need to put their names on the paper. The room became silent as everyone started writing. I watched carefully, making sure they had enough time.

Belenky et al. (1986)[3] found that the most powerful learning experiences for women were ones that helped them translate their ideas from the secrecy of private experience into a shared public language. Mothers usually named childrearing as the most powerful learning experience in their lives. They further maintain that the type of knowledge used in childrearing is typical of the kind of knowledge women value and schools do not. It is tuned into the concrete and particular, since mothering requires constant adaptive responses to changing situations.

When they finished writing, we had paired-sharing. They did not need to share anything that made them uncomfortable. I walked around the room, making sure everyone had a partner. I listened as the room went from a few quiet murmurings to animated expressive talking. I wanted to create a sense of safety, so I was careful to allow everyone privacy by keeping a respectful distance and making sure they had sufficient time. After giving them a few minutes' warning, I announced it was time to stop.

I discussed the gift we could all be for one another through sharing our own stories, since individually we all had limited experience. I asked if anybody was willing to share one of her experiences with the class. Nobody volunteered. I remained quiet, knowing that eventually somebody would gain the courage to speak. One brave woman finally raised her hand. She told about being 6 years old and left with a neighbor who constantly watched television. She was playing in the yard and tripped over a stone, cutting open her lower lip and chin. She needed stitches. Everyone was listening, some nodding with compassion. "It really scared me, and I learned never to leave a child alone when they are playing." She paused for a moment. "I'll tell you something. You'll never catch me just sitting around and talking like I see teachers doing all the time on playgrounds." Several students called out their agreement. Other people began sharing similar stories. I knew they all had more painful stories than these, but we had started developing a place together that we could trust.

We were ready to move on to other practical concerns. We began reviewing the syllabus. From previous classes I knew the isolation that students felt when they often did not understand many of the academic terms used in college. I began by defining the term "syllabus," adding that a lot of academic words are used in classes. I added a plea that few would respond to: "Please ask me about any words you do not understand."

Slowly and methodically, I went through the topics we would cover, the required schedules, attendance, assignments, and grading criteria. The room filled with tension. Nobody spoke a word. These were not students who had had many positive experiences in school. I reassured everyone that we would be reviewing these regularly. Anxiety remained. Beneath my words, I wanted them to know how much I cared about and respected them. We were settling in for the semester.

Many Roads to Learning

My new goals led me to a new kind of courage. And anxiety. I could not assume that I would always know what to do next. My desire for a responsive and dynamic learning environment required new skills. It demanded that I stay closely attuned to the students, the atmosphere of the class, and our collaboration. It meant making room for dialogue, honesty, and the spontaneous sharing of stories. It also meant deepening my own skills in observation and receptiveness.

I began paying close attention to how students were responding to me during the class. I paid particular attention to unspoken signals, ranging from nonresponsive silence and slumped bodies to alert interest and playfulness. Today, we were discussing common infectious diseases in young children. I mentioned the herpes virus showing up as cold sores around their mouths. Immediately there was an undercurrent of chatter as I talked. Finally, I stopped talking and smiled at everyone. Looking around the room, I called out, "Okay, come on back. Yes, it is also a sexual disease." They all started laughing, and then we talked more about it. I was discovering the importance of laughter and fun as part of our learning process.

Later in the class, I began sharing a personal story that was relevant to our topic. A person from the office came in and interrupted me. After he left, I forgot about it and continued with the class. A woman from the back of the room put her hand up and asked what I was going to say before the interruption. I couldn't remember. She wouldn't leave it alone. She said it was really important to hear what I was going to say. The whole class became silent while I tried to recall. Finally, I was able to begin the story again. They listened with interest and understanding as I talked about a situation in which I had faced an issue we were examining in the class. I could feel how attentive everyone had become and how much they valued the dialogue we had started.

The road of our learning was about to become a far more crooked path as the women began to feel safe in expressing their truth. While I was presenting a lecture on child abuse, I noticed a change in the students. Uncertain about what was happening, I continued with my definitions, statistics, and guidelines. As I finished, everyone in the class was tense and silent. Looking around, I said, "It is okay if you disagree with anything I just told you. An important job for us here is to talk about what we believe to be true. Let's break up into small groups and discuss the topic of child abuse, using these headings: (1) A clear case of child abuse, (2) A case that is not clear, and (3) A case you do not consider to be child abuse. For each of these include the reasons why you feel this way. Have one person do the writing."

In the safety of their groups, lively discussions began taking place. I had learned to be careful not to intrude, to stay mainly in the front of the room. After a while, I walked around checking to see if they had finished and gave them five more minutes. Each group was asked to share its examples and reasons. The whole class discussed the undecided cases. Although every group said that spanking was okay, they provided thoughtful criteria for its use or for any other kind of discipline that was considered acceptable.

I was amazed at the complexity of their understanding when they were allowed to voice opinions from their own experiences. One group became stuck in attempting to decide whether or not two situations were abuse. Two of the women in the group were raised by very strict mothers who spanked them as children. After much discussion and feedback from the rest of the class, they concluded that one would not be considered abuse, while the other one would. The first woman's mother was raising ten children by herself and working full time. She needed everyone to be well behaved and responsible at home and at school. Even though she was very strict and spanked them, she was also loving and affectionate. She made time for any of them when they needed it. The other woman's mother was also a single parent with a large family. But in addition to being strict and spanking them, she only spoke harshly to the children and was never affectionate or made time to talk with them. The class concurred that this was an abusive parent.

Throughout their sharing, I listened with new understanding. I thanked them for their honesty and sensitivity in the discussion and acknowledged that I had gained new insights myself. I reminded them that there was no one right way to live or to raise their children. Each of us must work this out for ourselves and our families. But as teachers, there are ways of disciplining children that they will need to understand and use. They nodded in agreement. It was a first step in expanding their awareness and in appreciating the validity of their experiences and opinions.

Recognizing the need for mutual learning in our class opened the door for real participation by the students. It also relieved me of the constant pressure of trying to force information on the students while ignoring their silent resistance. Elizabeth Jones (1993)[4] believes that in a rapidly changing and diverse society, the knowledge base of any one culture is inadequate to answer the questions that come up when cultures meet.

Regina talked of her ambivalence about being told she should use a different form of discipline with her child at home:

> I think a lot of stuff, let's say theory in books that I've heard. It does work in a sense. But it doesn't work, I say, if you have a child that you raised from birth to like 4 years old. And all you've known is to spank them. Right? And then you read a book that says...you shouldn't spank your children. You should give them a time-out or something. When you don't spank them, it is like really, "Oh...I didn't get whooped!" And so I'm going to do it again.

Paulo Freire (1997)[5] believes that authentic reflection focuses on real people as they experience the world. In this way, people develop their own power to perceive themselves in the world and make ongoing choices for their lives. They come to see the world and their own lives as in a process of transformation. I was beginning to discover the arrogance of thinking I had all the answers for everyone. It was clear that both the students and I were engaged in a process of growing together.

Reaching Out to One Another
There are times when one question or decision can take us into places we are not prepared to handle. For me, this began with a simple request. I asked the students to write their own definitions of "health" and describe a healthy child. The women all wrote and shared definitions fitting perfectly into standard textbooks and films: a family with two loving parents, a nice home and children well cared for, a child who gets all As in school.

As I listened to one definition after another, my own increasing awareness of the reality of these women's lives left me feeling helpless. I knew how far these definitions were from the truth of their lives and how these idealized portrayals of health could be affecting them. My distress continued for days, only getting worse as I thought about our educational films and the pictures in our textbooks.

During the next class, I decided to talk with the students about another dimension of health: the strength, compassion, and learning that can come out of painful experiences. Their written exercise on a painful event and what they learned from it were private. I told them they did not need to use their name or turn it in. When they finished, one woman after another began telling her story and the many ways she wanted to help deliver children and parents from the pain she had experienced. No bitterness. No self-pity. These were women committed to a mission, and their desire to help others was overwhelming.

Tears streamed down my face. Feeling embarrassed and disoriented, I desperately tried to regain my usual composure. I looked out at a room filled with loving faces. Then, one by one, they slowly started calling out, "It's okay to cry." As they left class, each woman came up and personally handed me her paper. Every paper included the woman's name. We were clearly taking this journey together.

Early the next morning, I started making the rounds to every office I could think of that offered help in basic skills in writing and in English as a Second Language. Reading their papers the night before, I was struck with the profound depth of their stories. I was also alarmed at the low level of basic English and writing skills of many students. I had expected this condition in my noncredit class and knew these students were all receiving help in this area. But this was different. This was a required credit-course with no preliminary requirements. A recipe for failure. How did this happen? Where were tutorial help and a writing center? Even in colleges where these alternatives exist, the students seemed unaware of them, were afraid of asking for help, or found the services to be inaccessible. Wasn't anybody paying attention to these students?

I thought of Lisa Delpit's plea that minority and poverty students need to learn the codes for participating fully in the mainstream of American life. She understood that learning basic skills meant starting with the basics: the cultural basics, the educational basics, the kind of practical language instruction that included classroom topics rooted in each student's life. I had two goals that morning: getting help that was easily accessible and creating meaningful assignments to use as the context for learning these skills. Arrangements were made to have several language-skills instructors speak to the class and explain the available services. Students now would have a place where they could concurrently work on content assignments and language skills.

I returned the papers that recounted painful experiences, having made narrative responses to the many thoughts and events they wrote about. No grammatical corrections yet. The purpose was thoughtful self-reflection. They would have other opportunities to work with writing skills. I announced to the class that this exercise would be expanded into an extra-credit assignment.

I was learning to use many ways to carry on responsive dialogues with students, including their written assignments. I decided to create a series of observation and self-reflection exercises to replace one of the larger assignments. This would give them an ongoing opportunity to connect their outside lives with class learning. And it would provide a meaningful structure for students to work on writing skills. The larger assignment could be worked on as part of a group in class. Next session we would discuss writing skills and the new assignments. Right now, we needed to savor our new level of connection with one another.

Stories and Learning

Rita came up to me before class. She told me about a tragedy that took place in her family that week. Still in shock, she kept saying that she could not believe this could happen to her family. Rita's niece is 21 years old, married, and has two children ages 5 years and 9 months. She is working and leaves the children at home with the father. Last Saturday, when she returned home in the afternoon the 9-month-old baby would not respond to her. The father would not say what happened. She called her father (Rita's brother), and he came over and took her and the baby to the hospital.

After they examined the baby, the police were called in to question the baby's father. Apparently, the father shook the baby so hard that his brain began hemorrhaging. They don't know how long the baby was left unattended after this happened. They flew the baby to another hospital and operated. They did not expect the baby to live. If he does, they said he would be blind and severely brain damaged. The mother was in a state of shock; the father was being held in custody, and the police took the 5-year-old out of the home till they investigated. Rita could not stop crying while she told me the story. She was also afraid for her brother who had a heart condition.

When she finished talking, Rita said she wanted to tell me before class started, because we were all learning from one another how to be better teachers and parents. She wanted everyone to hear this story so that they would be aware of the dangers of shaking a baby. She was afraid she would only cry if she tried to tell the class and asked if I would help her do it.

As Rita told her story, everyone listened in horror. The class discussed how common it is to shake babies, even when parents play with them. They talked about how they wanted to educate parents. Everyone discussed possible resources to help Rita and her family. Listening to the class, I realized the power of sharing real living experiences and that we had become a learning community.

The sharing of personal stories in class was an unusual occurrence for the women in this book. Those who had been in classes that incorporated this type of sharing found it to be their most powerful experiences in learning. Marcela talked about this type of experience:

> *It is a big difference of listening from everybody...from everybody's heart...from somebody's heart and tears than reading it in a book...those*

learnings cannot get them through the book. Because there is so much you can picture in a book. You can read your pain. But you will never see pain in these faces. And there was a time when somebody said, "Hey, you guys are doing great by trying hard." But the book will never tell you how hard you work. It won't ever say what is right in the book because those people didn't write the book for people who speak some other language.

Some progressive early childhood educators, such as Elizabeth Jones (1986),[6] promote interactive learning as part of their approach to teaching. She is concerned that contemporary education has become depersonalized and overmonitored by tests. She believes that such an approach comes at a high cost to the quality of learning.

One of the costs is the opportunity for genuine exploration of the women's real-life experiences that include complicated issues and no absolute answers. Carol Gilligan (1982)[7] discusses how our scientific approach to moral development devalues the traits that are important to women. She found that women do not make decisions according to abstract ideals with answers that can fit neatly on a test. Instead, they use a more complex mode that is expressed through discussions of true, concrete experiences. They continue to look at individuals, and their answers cannot be packaged.

Happy and Unhappy Endings

Even with these initial successes, this was not going to be a smooth road for any of us. As the semester continued, tragedies and illness struck some of the students, and others gave up from lack of skills. Yet, most flourished with a newfound sense of who they were as students and who they could become as teachers. Some students stood out in ways they had hardly dreamed possible.

A Happy Ending for Some

Chandra was an outstanding and dedicated student. In her mid-20s, she entered the room each day excited to be there, shared insightful stories about her two young children, and did excellent work on every assignment. She never missed a class. Halfway through the semester, Chandra was suddenly absent for four consecutive classes. I asked several students if they knew why she was not coming to class. Nobody had an answer.

When Chandra finally returned, she looked different. She appeared tired, and her typically impeccable clothing was rumpled. I asked if we could talk after class. When we were alone, Chandra profusely apologized for missing class and proceeded to tell me about the last month. When her landlord raised the rent, she could no longer afford to stay. A friend who was leaving the area for a year offered to rent her apartment to Chandra. Relieved to have a place, Chandra and her two children, ages 2 and 4 years, moved into their new home.

A few months later, the friend suddenly told her she was returning in two weeks and said that Chandra would have to leave. The family was now left homeless on the streets. They finally found a shelter, but both her children were falling apart emotionally and she had become depressed. Every day she prayed for guidance, and finally she began to see an answer. She thought about the exercise we did in class on getting stronger from painful experiences and using this knowledge to help others. Chandra realized that she needed to know about resources for housing, ways to get help, and places to go for assistance. She decided to make her experience with homelessness the subject for her extra-credit report. She started collecting information about all the available resources. Such knowledge was a lifeline for her and her family. Chandra showed me a notebook filled with brochures and resources that she was going to use to help other women in trouble. She and her children were still living in a shelter but were on a list for housing in the near future. With a new sense of purpose, Chandra decided to be a good example at the shelter and assist with any work that was needed. Her children were also adapting. She never missed another class. Several months later as the semester was ending, Chandra came to tell me she now had housing. Not all classroom stories ended so happily, but women like Chandra give hope.

No Clear Answers for Others
I was encouraged that the students were gaining access to many needed services available in the community. On this particular day, a guest speaker from a resource and referral agency had just finished her presentation. She then asked for questions. Dora, a student in her mid-50s, did not have a question. Instead, she told a sad and desperate story. She had worked for fifteen years as a bilingual aide, starting at $3.50 per hour. Eventually, she worked her way up to $10 per hour. Last summer,

she was told that she had to take six units in child development or lose her job. She tried taking the bus to school four nights a week, but it was too dangerous. So they fired her. Our guest speaker could only tell her that we now required more formal education.

Dora had not finished. She had a second story to share. Her daughter had a 1-year-old baby and had been using welfare to stay home and care for the baby. She was told to go to work as part of welfare reform. She finally found a babysitter she could afford, limited as she was by a minimum-wage job. Two days ago, the babysitter put Dora's granddaughter in hot water to take a bath, resulting in second-degree burns all over her body. She began shaking as she talked. There were no answers for this story.

Walking through campus the next day, I saw an ambulance parked near the library. Chills of alarm went through my body as I started running toward the library. The CalWORKS office (for welfare students) was upstairs. As I ran up the stairs, I hoped I was wrong about my fears. I asked the administrator what happened. She told me they just took Dora away in the ambulance. They think she had a heart attack.

Dora was a committed student who had struggled with written English. I assisted her in getting tutorial help with a basic skills instructor. She had been progressing well. Although she returned to school for a short time, she no longer had the physical and emotional strength to finish the semester. As was true of some other women in the class, the stresses of life had taken too great a toll.

Unanswered Questions
The stories in this chapter leave many unanswered questions. They tell only the beginnings of new possibilities for our teacher-preparation programs. It is the women themselves who can explore further what they want and need as students. Where do they find sources of strength as students? What is missing for them as students? What is detrimental to their progress and well-being as students? What works particularly well for them and why? What must we include in our college programs to support their learning, growth, and success?

Beyond the needs of students, other questions need exploration. How can we learn to effectively work with students of differing socioeconomic, cultural, racial, and religious backgrounds? How can we implement academic learning and still value spontaneous sharing and dialogue? What kinds of lesson plans, assignments, and criteria can be used that work for our students? What inner preparation is necessary to become more responsive and flexible with our students? How can we address our own anxiety as we explore previously unknown approaches of teaching? The following chapters begin addressing these new questions that demand new answers.

NOTES

1   Bloom, Paula J. *Avoiding Burnout: Strategies for Managing Time, Space, and People in Early Childhood Education.* Lake Forest, IL: New Horizons, 1982, and Cost, Quality, and Child Outcomes Study Team. *Cost, Quality and Child Outcomes in Child Care Centers.* Denver, CO: University of Colorado, 1995.

2   Noddings, Nel. "Stories in Dialogue: Caring and Interpersonal Reasoning." In *Stories Lives Tell: Narrative and Dialogue in Education* edited by Carol Witherell and Nel Noddings, 157–70. New York: Teachers College Press, 1991.

3   Belenky, Mary F., Blythe M. Clinchy, Nancy R. Goldberger, and Jill M. Tarule. *Women's Ways of Knowing: The Development of Self, Voice, and Mind.* New York: Basic Books, 1986. Through in-depth interviews with women, the authors explore ways that women are silenced in our classrooms and means for giving women a voice in their education. Among the many insights gained from this study, they found that women must first learn to hear their own inner voice in order to understand the importance of listening to others.

4   Jones, Elizabeth. Introduction to *Growing Teachers: Partnerships in Staff Development,* edited by Elizabeth Jones. Washington, DC: NAEYC, 1993. Through stories, this book shows the value of using a constructivist model for facilitating teachers' growth and learning.

5   Freire, Paulo. *Pedagogy of the Oppressed.* New York: The Continuum Publishing Co., 1997.

6   Jones, Elizabeth. *Teaching Adults: An Active Learning Approach.* Washington, DC: NAEYC, 1986. Jones presents a realistic picture of the challenges and rewards of using a constructivist approach to teaching adults.

7   Gilligan, Carol. *In a Different Voice.* Cambridge, MA: Harvard University Press, 1982. Gilligan conducted a pivotal study of women's moral development and the ways that their voice has been lost in standard educational theories and practices.

Chapter 6

In Their Own Words

Next week would be our last class session with all its final celebrations. A potluck list was already circulating around the room. Our first class began with introductions. Now it was time to say our good-byes. I decided to go around the room and ask each person to talk about her experience in class or anything else about her life this past semester. Unlike our introductions, everyone was nodding approvingly, and many smiled in response. I gave them some time to reflect upon what they wanted to share with the class.

Some students had little to say except for a quiet thank-you. Others spoke of difficulties they had overcome. Cristina remarked, "It was very difficult to learn so much new information and English at the same time." Then she added, "It was especially hard because I have six children and can only study late at night when everyone is asleep. But now I feel better 'cause I know I am strong. I even can help my children with their homework." Monique talked about how returning to school was threatening to friends and relatives. Her husband voiced this concern clearly when he said, "I'm afraid we are not the same anymore and we won't be equal."

Most surprising was hearing about the important role this class played in their personal well-being. The class had become a place of safety where they could venture out of a familiar world and discover new ideas and possibilities for their lives. They spoke of no longer feeling alone and of their gratitude for the security they experienced in the class. Sandra was typical in her comment, "This class was like my home. I felt free and accepted here even if I have made mistakes in my life." Renee said she looked forward all week to Thursday. Here she could be part of "a different world" that supported her in discovering new dreams.

Many told of becoming better parents and how they used the information at home. Leslie was proud that she knew what to do when her niece fell at a family gathering and broke her tooth. And how pleased her parents and sisters were that she was going to college. She ended with, "Nobody in my family ever did this."

Their oral sharing and written responses to both the "Mid-semester" and "End-of-the-Semester Comments" were invaluable sources for my own growth as a teacher. Students made suggestions and told which techniques worked and which ones failed. I realized how important it was to include feedback. Their remarks reinforced the importance of understanding our students beyond classroom appearances and exam scores. A year later, the women interviewed for this book would give extensive commentaries on their experience as students. They always began by discussing the types of learning that held the greatest value for them as students in early childhood education.

Our Most Valued Lessons

Angelica wanted to become a teacher, but this was not her immediate focus of interest as a student. She began taking classes in child development shortly after she had her first baby. Angelica was searching for guidance in her new role as a mother. When her own mother came to the United States, she had been left as a young child with an aunt and uncle in Mexico. Although they provided a caring home for her, Angelica wanted to be with her mother again. At 11 years old, she was reunited with her mother and a new stepfather in Los Angeles. This alliance resulted in abuse and virtual slavery for Angelica. She was regularly beaten and held responsible for cleaning, cooking, and caring for her younger stepbrother and sister. Somehow, she survived adolescence and young adulthood and finally found a happy life in her late 20s with her husband and baby. Angelica now had two goals: to be a good mother and to be a teacher for young children:

> *But after I had my baby I realized, I can help these children. And for myself, I wanted to learn. By taking these classes, I was going to learn how to teach my kid. How to treat my kid. Because I was in an abusing home, I didn't want to go through the circle again. And I wanted to be educated. I wanted to have patience for my kid. And this is going to help me a lot. I am more patient with my kid. I am now learning how to teach her. I didn't know how to, because I didn't have the time with my mom. She didn't teach me.*

The women talked repeatedly of the importance of using new insights and information to improve their lives as parents. These insights almost always came from classroom exercises of self-reflection and sharing among students. It was during this type of activity that Dimitria gained a new awareness that changed her relationship with her daughter. She was in a small group discussing personal experiences with disabled people when she suddenly realized her bias against her own daughter:

> *It gave me a chance to look at myself. Because I have a child that is disabled. And I had to look at, am I being too hard on her? Am I pushing her away? I was in denial. But today, I know that she has a disability and I live with it. And I treat her no different than the others. So learning some of the things and the techniques that this class had to offer have given me a different outlook on how to deal with disabled children.*

This interplay between classroom learning and parenting emerged from the very beginning. Rochelle was a student in a class that used many self-reflection exercises and home/community observations. Rochelle radiated her newfound awareness and a new confidence:

> *I enjoyed my class because there were some things I learned there as far as parenting and how to react to young children. Listening to them. Then paying attention to them. Spending time. Their ideas and thoughts are important. I am noticing that with my own young children. My youngest daughter, I have*

to pay attention to her. And I have to look at her. Just stop what I am doing to look at her.

Those who became teachers later recalled using these ideas in their classrooms. After an exercise exploring the importance of routine in her own adult life, Carmen discussed how she began making better use of routines with children in her class:

And I remember your CD 2 class. How you can implement a routine with small children. And you've been teaching us that if you are an adult, and you felt bad when you were getting out of the routine, how will the little ones feel?

Lakesha was not a parent, but she successfully applied a new approach for teaching math with the children in her class:

Child Development 4 is teaching them science and math. Because with the science and math where I am teaching now, I felt like the traditional ways of saying two plus two and putting it on the board was not helping the children. But Ms. Smith is teaching us to make different games for the kids so they will learn how to add but still have fun with it. When we have math activities due for her class, I take them to my class. And we learn the games and we play the games there. And it has helped them. And they really enjoy it now. They ask, "Ms. Lakesha, can we do math today? Can we play the game today?" Where it used to be, "Not math. Oh no, not the fingers again. Please don't put it on the board."

We discussed the value of a class that offers new information that students can actually apply. But it became more and more clear that the information was only a part of much more complex dynamics. Openness to learning and making use of this information depended primarily upon one factor: the teacher.

The Teacher Matters

The women discussed numerous topics as they reflected upon their college classroom experience. Overwhelmingly, the value of the class echoed the persona of the teacher. For college teachers, it is affirming to have our profession acknowledged in such a way, but it is a serious responsibility as well. I listened to Marcela describe her English writing-skills class.

It was a writing improvement; it was a class to make you be ready. In that class, I could not catch up; it was too fast. It was so much that you can't put in your head. With the people who fully, fully, fully speak English, probably. But mommies like me? Believe me, it was hard! It was everybody's concern. And it was everybody who got confused.

Yet, other women spoke of gaining great value from this same course with another instructor. For Ramona, developing these new skills became a key to success in her other classes:

English helps because now I like to write. So I like having those skills....I kind of write more. I mean it is better to make a report in other classes.

Dimitria's new ability in basic academic skills was also applied to her life as a parent:

I really enjoy my English class. I have gotten a lot out of it this semester. My writing has improved so much. My spelling has improved; my comprehension. It is just everything. And I've learned things that I didn't know about. And I really have something now that I can translate for my children when they need it.

What we are speaks louder than what we say, and effective lesson plans are only half the lesson. Student responses continued to affirm the need for the college instructor to be a role model of compassion and flexibility, the very traits these students would need when they became teachers of young children. Sharnette talked of how she views a college instructor in our field:

If you have compassionate teachers, they are setting an example for you. As our children learn, and I believe that is how adults learn too, is by setting examples. Having a nice teacher that is compassionate and understanding makes you feel safe.

For Rosa, the teacher's attitude and lack of explanations left her with little motivation to study or do well in the class:

I think it all depends on the teacher that teaches it. She just always had an attitude. She would just look at us up and down...like, oh, she looks better than we do. You come to school to learn and to have a teacher like that? You are not going to learn nothing. Just nobody liked her. If you didn't get it, oh

well! "That is what you have your book for. Go read it." She would not go
back and explain things. Nobody liked her.

In contrast, Irma described a teacher who presented the requirements and course content clearly to the students. In particular, this
teacher appreciated the students' readiness to ask questions and their
active engagement in the learning process:

> *Child Development 2. It was different. I mean she would give us study guides.*
> *She would go over the chapters every time, every single time....Ask us*
> *questions. Ask us if we understand. What we think. What our comments are.*
> *You could talk about it. You could have comments. You had questions. That*
> *made it more interesting. More interesting, yes. But when you don't get that,*
> *you feel bored. Or you misunderstand some things. Or you just don't ask*
> *questions. And this one I like because we made reports. We read. And we had*
> *group time. We shared. We practiced. I mean, when you are active...doing*
> *different things, the class is more interesting. You learn.*

These responses began opening the door to my greater awareness
of what makes a classroom experience valuable. As our interviews continued, I also became aware of unmet needs for the women. I
discovered that significant gaps centered around areas of personal
identity, self-worth, and their relationships with others. These missing
elements permeated all dimensions of their educational experience. For
programs designed to prepare students to successfully work with the
complicated human relations of supporting the lives of children and
families, these gaps were particularly disturbing.

The women's reflections provide valuable insights for needed improvements. Our approach to teacher preparation will either enhance or
diminish our students' ability to deal effectively with complex life
issues. The quality of education we provide for our students will bring a
commensurate sense of who they are and will define their ability to
connect with others in their work as teachers.

The Loud Voice of Silence
In any academic setting, we teach our students many lessons beyond
the syllabus. The women often commented on the silent messages they
received throughout their time as students. A lack of support and
guidance during the critical beginning period of our program speaks

loudly to our new students. Lakesha discussed her entrance into early childhood education:

> *You need to know where to start. And I didn't know where to start. They didn't have counseling at all. So I was taking like Child Development 2 and Child Development 11, but I hadn't taken Child Development 1. And a lot of students have done that. Because it is really difficult, not knowing how to take the classes...I don't think that they explain that enough. So I had to drop the class and just start back over at 1. And then work my way up.*

For Lakesha the system or lack of it had delayed completion of educational requirements. But for many of the women, the lack of assistance went deeper than confusion, lost units, and delays. It sent a message that they were not welcome in this institution. Unspoken and oh-so-familiar negative attitudes routinely surfaced toward these students. Their socioeconomic level and weak language skills had labeled them as candidates who simply weren't ready. Carmen described the message she received:

> *You know, sometimes you see kind of a racism. Because you are coming from Cuba. Or you are coming from Colombia. Or from Mexico. And then you feel like in your heart you are not ready for this! And the way they are talking to you. Just be fair. But do not make exceptions like, "Okay, you know, you are not going to be in the program." Just because of your color. Because of your hair. Because of your skin. Because of your eyes. Or maybe because you don't have enough money. And if the college can prepare any kind of program, I am saying, just be consistent.*

Few of the women were aware of the possibility of becoming part of a supportive environment connected to their education. Although Carmen spoke of feeling "completely lost," she was typical in her lack of expectation of an orientation for new students. When I mentioned this idea, her face lit up with enthusiasm:

> *Oh yes, yes, that would be wonderful. Because even myself and other students that I know, I felt at the beginning like I was lost! And some students, when they are coming from high school—they just felt lost!*
>
> *I don't know what to study. I don't know where do I have to go. Special orientation would be wonderful.*

Once again, I realized the importance of listening to our students' concerns and of finding possible solutions. As the women continued their discussion about entering college, they began addressing other challenges that often left them with a profound sense of isolation.

Building upon Strength and Commitment

A new sense of enthusiasm rose as they addressed and searched for solutions to other serious problems. One such challenge is the crisis in personal identity faced by many nontraditional students entering our programs. Rosemary spoke of the importance of encouragement as they risk trusting in a new future:

> *I think it is very valuable for a person to know that they are not out there by themselves. And let them know that they can make it. There is still hope today. That they can build their lives up.*
>
> *And I am a firm believer that everybody needs to have words of encouragement. People need that. You know, people fall. People get up. People fall again. And it is okay. But you know, in all of these falls, there is something that you must have learned.*

Amid our textbooks, films, and classroom learning, we are preparing our students for lives of service. We want them to leave our college programs prepared to help children and parents in our society. This daunting task requires making themselves visible to others and believing they have something of worth to offer. Skills and information are helpful but not sufficient for becoming a person of service to our society.

With nothing from their past lives to build upon, students' personal identity becomes only a source of hidden shame. We need to ask ourselves, what can bridge the gap for these students? How can we help them to stand tall as they face this new learning environment that initially leaves them feeling unprepared and out of place? Kaufman (1980)[1] found that the key to healing a sense of shame comes through caring and authentic communication in which one's unique identity is respected and valued.

The teacher that Irma remembered with such awe is a wonderful model for all of us. We could begin by making use of guidelines already developed in our field. Joanne Hendrick (1996),[2] in a book commonly used in teacher preparation classes, describes good human relationships as the fundamental ingredient for an effective early childhood program. Warmth, empathetic understanding, and genuine caring for each child as a unique person are considered the most influential factors for an environment that promotes healthy adjustment and openness to learning. College instructors simply need to apply these same principles to their adult students who are struggling with the uncertainties of beginning a new path.

Maslow (1968)[3] recognized that new learning always requires the risk of letting go of the safety of previous answers. He found the need for acceptance and safety exists for all human beings when faced with this risk. He believes two sets of forces are operating within everyone. One set clings to safety out of fear, and the other set impels them forward toward growth. "Assured safety permits higher needs and impulses to emerge and to grow towards mastery" (p. 49).

Orientation is a must. Even for the most confident among us, a new environment feels threatening. We cannot take for granted that all students know of available services, program sequence, and department requirements. The orientation program can create confidence, provide security, impart practical information, and establish dialogue among new students, faculty, counselors, and experienced students. When necessary, appointments can be scheduled for special-needs situations. The benefits of a thoughtfully managed orientation program are immeasurable for all of us.

For women in poverty, building a support system to connect with others who have been through similar experiences is more than just a nice endeavor. Sharnette poignantly described how this could be a lifeline for these women:

> *It will give them a sense of hope. It shows them that other women have done it. And understanding goes a long way when you've been through stuff like that. And I believe it will give them pride. It will give them their life back. Sharing experiences can give you that. It gives you a reason to live. It builds up your self-esteem, your self-discipline; it shows you that there is a way out of hell.*

Our orientations can begin a system of support that breaks the isolation of leaving one world behind and becoming an outsider in the new world. Sharing breaks through the isolation. An acknowledgment of the vision that brought them to this program gives birth to new hope.

An introductory class offers the needed direction. It offers that "sense of hope" that Sharnette remembered so well. It provides the needed bridge for a fragile population to pursue postsecondary education.

Building upon Who We Are
The introductory class can be designed to create a caring community of students sharing a common purpose. It can be a model for the kind of supportive environments these same students can create for the young children in their future classrooms. It is not a myth that lives of service have a boomerang effect. Forgiveness brings healing, and helping others helps oneself.

Introductory classes provide a pivotal opportunity for the students who need this kind of beginning. Although an argument can be made that academic credit provides the indisputable benefit of higher motivation, needed units, and a sense of achievement, my offering did not include credit. There were different advantages to a noncredit class. The students were free from risks associated with grades and failure. The pace was relaxed, but the goals remained clear. This class was the dress rehearsal for the full-credit college program that they aspired to. A departmental certificate of completion for the class added to its educational validity. My work with this introductory class reaped more benefits than I ever would have thought possible.

The class introduced basic concepts of early childhood education through observational and self-reflective assignments. Bridging the gap between personal and educational lives, these assignments were based on observations in familiar settings, such as their homes, neighborhoods, or public parks and playgrounds. The assignments also included personal reflections about students' own lives.

Through the writing and sharing of these assignments, students experienced a new validity to their values and opinions. They felt confidence, even a certain sense of authority. They spoke; they listened; they were listened to. Jones (1993)[4] believes that everyone entering our field brings relevant experiences with young children, starting with their own childhood. Human development offers many opportunities for telling personal stories. Whether we are examining self-esteem, temperament, divorce, immigration, communication, race or religion, students can contribute stories that capture their living experience. Sharing and reflecting upon these experiences in the classroom help to form a foundation for combining teaching theory and practice.

The introductory class concept allows students to go beyond developing individual competencies and enables them to explore their pasts through multicultural lenses. Each self-reflective and observational experience enhanced the women's sense of competence and built new bonds among them. Without personal sharing, the teacher runs the risk of making the textbook the single tool. Lisa Delpit (1995)[5] wrote of her concern that our failure to allow student stories will produce only a mindless imitation of other people's beliefs rather than a reflection on teaching as an interactive process.

The assignments in this class can be as all-embracing as the teacher's imagination can conceive. Tutorial work with a writing-skills instructor can become part of the program. Implementation of new introductory classes can be the beginning of new pedagogical practices and unprecedented academic successes for those students who are reaching out to us.

The Power of Being Heard

As the powerful force of learning about themselves unfolded for these women, a dramatic shift in their identity began to emerge. They saw themselves as capable learners. They recognized the value of their own instincts. Some of them were experiencing respect for the first time in their lives. Observing the remarkable benefits for women in the introductory classes, I realized the healing power of being heard. Not only were the women grasping complex ideas with great depth, remarkable changes in their self-concept were evidenced. Using personal stories and home/community observations generated abundant confidence, and they contributed their own unique perspective to all our discussions.

This principle was also manifested in the women interviewed for this book. Diane arrived early for her second interview. So had two other women, and one brought a large picture of her family to show me. When the fourth woman showed up thirty minutes early and watched for my arrival, I added a question. "How was it for you—telling me about your life?" Regina's face lit up as I asked her:

> *I really liked it because it helped me look at myself. Because you don't usually talk about yourself day to day. I feel that the way other people look at*

you, it should be who you are. And what you've been though in your life.
Because I don't believe in people judging other people. And it also helped me
when I go on childcare interviews, to talk freely about the things I believe in.

Lakesha was finally able to break through her fears and no longer
had to be secretive about her time spent in jail:

It just relieved a lot of stress, because since I want to be a teacher I am going
to have to keep going over, "Well, why did this happen and what happened
here?" I guess at first I was more afraid to talk about it. But now I am really
just open with it. Because I've changed my life around from that point. And
I'm doing such positive things now.

Dimitria gained a larger perspective of her life as being a process of
learning rather than feeling shame about her past:

When I did that interview with you, it just opened me up. It allows me to go
back and see how blessed I am. It was helpful to define myself. It allows me
to go back and see where I was and where I'm at today. It keeps me focused.
And what a difference!

Female educators have explored the healing process that takes
place for women when they begin to share their life stories.
Noddings (1991)[6] believes that including such stories as part of
education is to take seriously the quest for life's meaning as well as
the meaning of individual lives. It joins self-understanding and life
experiences. It was this level of learning that was missing from the
women's education.

Preparation for Real Living

Sharnette's face became thoughtful and serious as she searched for
ways to express what she felt was lacking in our programs. She
described her neighbor, a woman now completing her child
development certificate at a community college:

One of the neighbors that I have, she works for a childcare in LA Unified.
And I don't know how she is in her class with the kids. But with her nephew
that she has at home, she is such a bitch. She's mean. She's rude. She is not a
nice person...she is not physically abusive but she is verbally abusive,
emotionally abusive. And that type of person I don't think should be involved
with kids.

*She had a term paper due for CD 22. She copied everything out of the book.
She is not learning anything. And I know for a fact the only reason she wants
to do it because it was an easy job. So some people who go into it for the
wrong reason and just learn the book work and get the degree and not care.
And for the well-being of the children and what's best for the children, you
have to have people that care about children.*

The majority of women expressed concerns that our focus on book
learning, written tests, and papers does not adequately prepare students
as teachers. Although the women gained value from new information,
they repeatedly spoke of the need for their education to extend beyond
receiving information.

Several women suggested requiring observations and work with
children as an ongoing part of the program. Regina wanted this type of
experience to enhance the learning process. She included a possible
way to implement her ideas:

*I think basically we should work more on hands-on than book, rather than
just book most of the time. Every week bring in a few children and observe
and watch them play and interact with them. And we will better understand
how they are. Say we are on development. And you bring in children and you
look for that basic thing. And every week it is different. You learn different
stuff. You observe different stuff. And you understand better.*

Monitoring the field was another reason for including direct work
with children. Dimitria recommended that students spend a specific
number of weeks working in the field. In this way, they could find out
if they really want to work with young children:

*People going into child development should have, before they leave, a
certificate for volunteering in a daycare. And maybe having one on the
campus where even some parents could bring their kids. And let them
volunteer so many hours of watching these children. Just get the experience.
Three weeks will let you know if you really want to get into child
development. I know some people who said, "I want to work with kids. I love
kids. I love kids." And after they are around them so long, "Well, I can't deal
with these kids!" So you really have to have in your heart, to know that you
want to deal with these children.*

Diane described the need to expand our approach to education to
include personal qualities that are vital to their work as teachers:

In order to really reach people, we have to work with more than just intellect. That is important—reading, writing, and being able to be successful on a job and so on. But I mean knowing how to speak to people, knowing how to carry yourself, and just be the best person you can be. That is also important. And in a lot of schools, I don't see it as much. And that is another concern that I have.

Failure to incorporate these dimensions of personal interaction in our academic models of teaching is particularly damaging for women. Carol Gilligan (1982)[7] became aware that women's perspectives are missing from most of our psychological theories. She realized that both our theories and teaching practices reinforce women's beliefs that they should be passive and silent. Women communicate most effectively when they are able to include emotions as well as thoughts; they value active listening. When there is no place for this type of communication, the feminine voice becomes silent.

In a field that is 98% female, such theories and practices have serious consequences for our students. They do not prepare them for the demanding situations they will be facing with children and parents. Noddings (1991)[8] found our masculine, scientific mode of logico-mathematical reasoning to be antithetical to the dynamics of inter-personal reasoning. Interpersonal reasoning is based on being open, flexible, and responsive. It values relationship over a particular outcome and is based on connection rather than separation and abstraction.

Regina talked about the difference of being in a class that included personal sharing:

So this has been the first class where I really enjoyed it. I mean before, you might be in a class with a lot of people and never know nobody. So I really think that it is good to talk about who you are and what you've been through. I looked at myself. And it just made me feel okay.

This sense of safety and acceptance often opened the door for the women to bring up frightening issues that needed to be heard by others in the class.

A Pedagogy for Connection and Learning

Silvia listened intently to our class discussion on ways a teacher can make a difference with parents as well as children. She suddenly raised her hand to speak. Looking frightened, she stood up in search of greater courage. "I want you to know about a teacher who changed my life." Silvia began telling about a teacher in a Head Start program who noticed that Silvia's daughter seemed very depressed. Her little girl would not play and always seemed sad. Silvia knew why but could not tell anyone.

Silvia had three young children, was married, and living in poverty. She began describing her husband's increasing abuse of her and the children. She talked about becoming so "unsteady" in her thinking that she had not even noticed her children. The teacher kept talking with her and trying to find out what was happening in her home. After several months, she told Silvia she thought she was a wonderful and courageous woman and mother. Hearing this, Silvia broke down sobbing and told her story. The teacher called social services and an investigation followed.

Her husband was furious that Silvia had told an outsider. But for Silvia, her silence had been broken, and she was able to take action. She moved into a shelter, leaving her husband and taking the three children with her. Two weeks later, he begged her to come back. They went into counseling and there has been no abuse since that time. She ended by saying that she plans on helping other women in situations like hers, because she understands what it is like.

Every woman in the class listened with rapt attention. Silvia's detailed descriptions, including her shame and inability to talk to anyone, gave a vivid portrayal of abuse. We discussed this topic for the rest of class, and everyone said she now truly understood abuse for the first time.

Marcela never forgot Silvia's story and named it as her most powerful learning experience. She described the importance of sharing personal experience as opposed to readings in a book:

> So I think we learn from everybody. And those learnings cannot get them through the book. Because there is only so much you can picture in a book. So I think by saying the experiences, by living, by coming and saying this is what happened to me. "I don't want it to happen to you." You just know that you are going to be ready. And so I value those classes. I value the opportunity of all of us sharing. It make you aware. It make you understand. It make you feel what pain is all about.

Silvia's courage in telling her story did more than convey important information. It brought a new level of self-worth, critical thinking, and connection to every woman in the class. It gave everyone a new voice and, with it, a new sense of power and identity. Belenky et al. (1986)[9] found that for many oppressed women, words have been used as a weapon against them. Sometimes they were punished for speaking. It is through the use of stories that these women come back to a kind of knowing that had been silenced by the institutions and society.

Since our programs are preparing students for a field based on relationships, we need to move well beyond statistics and standardized information. Yet, Jersild (1955)[10] found the prevailing tendency in education encouraged "the learner to understand everything except himself" (pp. 81–81).

We need to model how to interact with people, particularly those facing difficult transitions. The ability to respond compassionately is essential for teachers of young children. Through practices of observation, inner reflection, and authentic sharing, our classrooms are enhancing students' intuitive capacities and the compassion that comes from direct connection with another person (Noddings and Shore, 1984).[11] Sylvia's intuitive understanding of a desperate mother enabled her to move beyond superficialities and build upon a caring relationship. Our lesson plans need to include feelings.

The college teacher needs to scan her classroom to learn just what it is that builds and enhances each student. For every woman, bringing her own life into our classrooms was the genesis of learning. Yet, this emphasis is not part of the official canon of education. I have found that most standard pedagogical practices concentrate on external information with little or no focus on the individual student.

For Dimitria, sharing personal experiences in an atmosphere of safety brought a sense of security and motivation:

> It is good to reunite with people that are going in the same direction. Who have been through what you have been through. And who let me know that "Hey, it's okay." I'm still okay. You are okay. It allows each individual to just be themselves. With more self-esteem, pride. And they begin to feel motivation.

For Ramona, a focus on personal sharing brought the added benefit of a new sense of connection with others as students:

You wanted the students to express themselves, to give their own experiences. And a lot of them did. And that made us feel more comfortable with each other. So I really enjoyed your class because you wanted students to open themselves up to experiences so we could learn from it and be better teachers. Or be better people, I think.

The best teacher education programs prepare our students to face complicated and changing situations in their work with children and families. They will need to respond to human complexity in a way that is personal and realistic. It was this level of teaching that the women praised. And it is this level of teaching that is neglected. We need to discover new ways of teaching that address life itself.

NOTES

1   Kaufman, Gershen. *Shame: The Power of Caring*. Cambridge, MA: Schenkman Publishing Co. Inc., 1980.

2   Hendrick, Joanne. *The Whole Child*, 7th ed. Englewood Cliffs, NJ: Prentice Hall, Inc., 1996.

3   Maslow, Abraham. *Toward a Psychology of Being*. New York: Van Nostrand Reinhold Company Inc., 1968. Maslow explores a broader picture of healthy development and learning that includes both positive and negative experiences.

4   Jones, Elizabeth. Introduction to *Growing Teachers: Partnerships in Staff Development,* edited by Elizabeth Jones. Washington, DC: NAEYC, 1993.

5   Delpit, Lisa. *Other People's Children: Cultural Conflict in the Classroom*. New York: The New Press, 1995.

6   Noddings, Nel. "Stories in Dialogue: Caring and Interpersonal Reasoning." In *Stories Lives Tell: Narrative and Dialogue in Education,* edited by Carol Witherell and Nel Noddings, 157–70. New York: Teachers College Press, 1991.

7   Gilligan, Carol. *In a Different Voice*. Cambridge, MA: Harvard University Press, 1982.

8   Noddings, "Stories in Dialogue," 157–70.

9   Belenky, Mary F., Blythe M. Clinchy, Nancy R. Goldberger, and Jill M. Tarule. *Women's Ways of Knowing: The Development of Self, Voice, and Mind.* New York: Basic Books, 1986.

10 Jersild, Arthur T. *When Teachers Face Themselves*. New York: Teachers College Press, 1955.

11 Noddings, Nel, and Paul J. Shore. *Awakening the Inner Eye: Intuition in Education*. New York: Teachers College Press, 1984. This book examines the critical role of intuition in learning and ways to support its use in our classrooms.

Chapter 7

Our Lives as Instructors

It was in my fifth-grade class that I first realized the powerful role a teacher plays in a student's life. This was a special class for me. The kiln in the corner of the room held particular fascination. I waited eagerly for the day we would get to do ceramic artwork. The teacher finally announced that we would be making ashtrays. I sat entranced looking at my piece of wet clay. Carefully, I molded it beneath my fingers and watched it form into a smooth, round shape. I would make it bright blue and give it to my Aunt Mildred for her birthday. So absorbed in my work, I hardly heard the bell ring at the end of the day. We left our ashtrays to be baked in the kiln.

I decided not to tell anyone at home about my ashtray. It would be a surprise. Practically running to school the next day, I held my breath, waiting to see it. The teacher picked up one lovely ashtray after another, carefully handing one to each student. Finally, everyone was holding a new ashtray to take home. Everyone, that is, except for me.

Looking around, I suddenly froze in my seat. The teacher was walking up to the front of the room holding the leftover pieces of my blue ashtray. She sternly announced, "One person did not make her ashtray as instructed, and it blew up in the kiln." Displaying the broken pieces, she told everyone that this is what happens when you don't follow directions. Filled with horror and shame, I desperately tried not to cry. Finally, the bell rang, signaling it was time to go home. I couldn't run away from that school fast enough, and I sobbed all the way home. My secret ashtray would never be seen by anyone.

Decades later, another incident provided the opportunity for me to explore this influential dynamic between teachers and students in our classrooms. The director of the GAIN[1] program at a community college offered me a class teaching fifteen immigrant women who had tested at a low level for academic and English competency skills. This would be a noncredit course.

I arrived feeling excited and well prepared to teach the class. I brought in a student worker to help translate. I had planned some simple activities for getting acquainted and introducing my new students to the field. The women were seated, cautiously watching me. After a short introduction, I announced our first activity: "Tell us your name, a special event from your childhood, and one thing you would enjoy as a teacher." I listened as each woman responded with only her name and the length of time she had lived here. Puzzled by the lack of response, I tried another activity that produced a similar response. These were simple exercises. What was wrong with these people?

An hour into the session, my initial excitement was replaced by annoyance and frustration. The women barely responded to anything. I felt trapped in an impossible situation. This was a college classroom, and we had material to cover. How easy did I have to make the course? How much would I have to lower academic standards for these students? I left the room with a terrible headache, never wanting to return.

I also left haunted by the memory of my fifth-grade teacher. I remembered the angry look on her face and my silent devastation. Did she know that she was breaking my spirit along with the broken pieces of ceramic? I knew I had this same power. I watched the women's faces fill with fear and uncertainty as they saw my frustration. I knew their increasing silence represented one more broken dream in their lives.

Most distressing was my growing awareness that the problems in this class were only a more severe version of those present in other early childhood courses. I had talked with instructors as I tried to find ways to get students to understand foreign concepts and vocabulary, to complete requirements, and pass the tests. I watched frightened students struggling with complicated textbooks, trying to keep up with assignments they did not understand. I didn't have answers, but I knew there had to be a way out of this struggle.

Reconsidering Priorities

Where do we turn when our textbooks and lesson plans stop working? What do we do with curricula designed for students so different from those we face in class? Madeleine Grumet (1988)[2] provided some insights into the core of many self-defeating practices faced by college instructors in our field. She found that most teachers are women, yet teaching remains in a male-based mode. I thought of my own frustration in attempting to apply lesson plans covering extensive curriculum data, while fighting for extra minutes needed to create an atmosphere that supports human relationships. These constraints became even more costly in my work with students who were already struggling with basic competencies and a second language.

With this new class of immigrant women, my usual attempts to follow a prescribed curriculum became impossible. As I tore up my carefully prepared semester plans, I knew I needed to find answers beyond the constraints of the current agenda. Where could I look for new guidelines?

I thought of my fifth-grade teacher who had taught me more than ceramics. I remembered the feelings of shame and inadequacy. We can all recall times when we felt misunderstood, defeated, or rejected as students. We can also remember moments when learning felt like magic, and we experienced the gift of having a teacher who truly cared about and understood us. Recapturing those moments can help make us the teacher we want to be, the kind of teacher remembered by so many of the women in this book.

I looked at the guidelines that exemplify our field. Early childhood textbooks emphasize the importance of encouraging children to play a dynamic role in their own learning. They discuss the foundation of meaningful learning as emerging from life experiences of children. The research documents that children's sense of self crystallizes when they are respected for their uniqueness and their value to the class. These principles apply to learners of all ages, yet they remain an untapped resource for adult students.

For many nontraditional women in our teacher preparation classes, a sense of empowerment is a particularly critical issue. As teachers in childcare programs, these women will need to have confidence and the ability to respond effectively to complex and unpredictable situations. In her research on effective teachers, Elizabeth Jones (1993)[3] found that a self-fulfilling prophecy takes place when teachers are respected by colleagues and valued for their skill and imagination. They discover leadership and reach levels that they had never deemed possible. This same dynamic takes place for students in our teacher preparation classes. The journey of all of our students must begin with respect and encouragement. Especially for the teacher of nontraditional students, flexibility is everything. The teacher must be willing to nurture dreams. Dreams that spiral upward need to be the real agenda.

People Come First
When English skills are minimal, we must begin with a different basis for learning. We cannot solely depend upon books, films, and lectures as a method of teaching. At the end of our first session, I gave the women an observational homework assignment. I asked them to observe their children in two types of play situations: (1) when they were upset with one another and (2) when they were happily playing together. I wanted them to describe how they could tell whether or not the children were getting along.

The next week the women were again watching me with great caution. I went around the room asking each person to share her observations. This time they had experiences from home to bring into the class. They tentatively began talking about watching their children play. The women became increasingly animated as they described their children. When I asked them to illustrate in more detail how they could tell whether or not the children were playing happily, several women began imitating the faces and body movements of their children. After a while we were all laughing together. I discussed the importance of observing body language with young children, acknowledging their ability to see these signals as a vital form of communication. Everybody was showing excitement for the first time.

When the students began connecting their personal lives to classroom learning, they discovered their own voice. They found that they had been doing research for a good part of their lives. Nel Noddings (1984)[4] believes that our highest priority in teaching must be caring for each student as a unique person. One way of demonstrating this concern is through a partnership. Subject matter must be taught through the eyes of the students as well as through those of the teacher. If this element is missing, the student becomes little more than an inanimate object, a dispensable part of a formula.

We often fear that too much emphasis on human relationships will diminish academic learning. By contrast, I was relieved that the women were showing me the importance of new approaches to learning. But change comes at a cost. My desire for an exciting and vibrant classroom was leading me into difficult choices with no clear road map. Should I try to cover the entire textbook? And what about the more sensitive topics, the ones with no clear solutions? What if students get emotional over certain topics? What if I get emotional?

In the coming years, these were the challenging questions I needed to address in restructuring my approach to teaching. In the meantime, the fears were overshadowed by the vision of my classroom as I wanted it to be.

The Living Classroom
What is it about the sharing of food, that oldest form of hospitality, that brings people together? For my Thursday morning child development class, coffee and pastry were made available for the students. These students had held jobs in Head Start programs and had acquired some practical experience and a bit of confidence. This new academic road, however, would be arduous. It was unfamiliar territory and utterly frightening. It placed new restraints on their lives, which were already burdened with responsibilities and economic stress. Reassuring beginnings were important. The food helped.

Arriving to teach the class one morning, I sensed that something was slightly out of tune. I carefully scanned the room. Nothing looked different. Everyone was present, waiting to begin. I took attendance, still wondering. Finally, I asked what was wrong. One woman spoke with embarrassment: "The coffee machine is not working. The coffee is lukewarm and tastes like water." I announced that we would begin class by taking a fifteen-minute break so they could walk over to McDonald's and get a cup of coffee to bring back. When they returned, everyone was alert, smiling, and ready to begin. They also brought me coffee and refused to let me pay. We were learning our first lesson of the morning, the importance of paying attention to needs in others and to life's little rituals.

I needed to refine my skills in observing classroom dynamics. The short-term benefits would be evident in my own classroom, and the long-term benefits would reach the classrooms of these future teachers. We learn by modeling others. So much is taught between the lines of the scheduled agenda.

In an effort to adjust the curriculum to the student, I began allowing the amount of time spent on topics to vary, depending upon their importance and the nature of response from students. Issues that created intense interest and in-depth discussions were given more time. Other topics were covered with brevity, and some I chose to eliminate.

I began our new topic on parenting issues in the modern family with a personal story. It was a story that reflected my own unrealistic expectations about family life. My husband and I were living in northern California when our first child was born. My mother was planning to fly up from Los Angeles to help with the baby. We told her not to plan on coming up for the first week, since we wanted to spend a romantic week alone with our new baby. Three hours after arriving home, exhausted and panic-stricken, we were making emergency calls to my mother to take the next flight up. My opening "lecture" was clearly understood: How readily we embrace the idealized, but false, image.

After a few more introductory remarks on some of the key issues modern families face, I asked the class to work in groups. Each group was to discuss challenges they had experienced as parents, giving a personal example of three different issues. Animated discussions began, and some students became emotional as they described difficulties they have faced as parents.

When we reconvened, I asked each group to select two stories to share with everyone. The stories were kept anonymous, unless the person chose otherwise. Every student was listening with great interest. This was about their own lives. It was easy to relate to all issues—from confusion, loneliness, and guilt to satisfaction, deep love, and much new learning. We went from laughter to concern as each story revealed personal struggles and triumphs. Throughout the discussion, we explored ways that we as teachers could support parents and children. The key factor everyone agreed on: the need for role models who were compassionate and nonjudgmental listeners.

We were practicing with one another these very skills they would need as teachers. A number of times students criticized behavioral guidelines from their textbook, guidelines that seemed remote and simplistic. Several mothers who had been through a divorce while their children were still young felt there were too many unrealistic recommendations for a parent in this type of crisis. As one woman said, "I was so upset, I could barely get through the day. It would not have helped me to hear a list of ten things I needed to do for my children." We then brainstormed and came up with five important guidelines they felt would be most helpful for a parent going through a divorce.

Carter and Curtis (1994)[5] in their teacher training workshops found that teachers must unlearn many traditional roles in order to respond to our increasingly complex social, political, and technological realities. From years of experience, we have all been deeply ingrained with the "correct" role of a teacher. As I had learned in my fifth-grade class, the traditional role too often prescribed the answers and did not take risks. Teachers need to embrace risk, dialogue, and new ideas. By constructing knowledge from their own experience, the women in class were able to practice new skills and assume a more responsive role with children and parents. It also enhanced their sense that they have the capacity to help others.

Making a Difference in Our World

The women interviewed in this book all spoke of a passionate mission to help others through their work as teachers. This commitment must be recognized and encouraged in our classrooms. As a college instructor, bell hooks (1994)[6] realized that she could not have an exciting class if everyone was shut down emotionally. It left no room for the true passion that needs to be an integral part of the learning process.

Using personal stories as part of our curriculum took the class beyond the emotional neutrality associated with education. Their stories brought them back to the intense emotional impact of the struggles we all face as human beings. These stories also brought a deeper meaning to the important nature of their work as teachers. Jersild (1955)[7] believes this search for meaning is the most significant and fundamental task for human beings. It is a search that is distinctly personal, "not just a scholarly enterprise" (p. 6). Effective teacher preparation needs to build upon the intrinsic commitment and experiences students bring into our programs.

As part of our discussion on teacher support for parents, I asked the students to do a personal reflection exercise. They were to think of a time when another person had made a significant difference in their lives. I asked them to describe what was happening, who made the difference, and what this person did that was of such value to them. As the women quietly reflected and wrote, several began to cry. I did not interfere with anybody during this period of time, except to quietly offer a tissue. They had the option of paired sharing. A few women chose to speak to the whole class about their experience. These were intensely emotional moments for the speaker as well as for the listeners. But at this stage in our development as a class, we were ready.

Several weeks later, Teresa shared a story that took place in a Head Start program in which she was an aide. She told of a young single parent of three children who had a daughter in the program. Her daughter contracted head lice, and the mother did not take the proper measures to get rid of it. The school authorities had to keep sending the child home. Furthermore, the parent was not providing required paperwork to the school. The teachers became exasperated and wanted to dismiss her and the child from the program.

When Teresa decided to talk with this mother, she discovered that this woman was a victim of unspeakable circumstances. After a pregnancy when she was 14 years old, her family disowned her. Now with two more children, she was living alone and working to take care of her family. She used public bus transportation to bring them to school and go to work. Overburdened with personal struggles, she was unable to respond to written requests from Head Start. Teresa patiently explained to the woman what she needed to do to get rid of the lice and how to finish the paperwork. Teresa said that after our discussions in class, she knew that it was unfair to just label and judge this woman. I was reminded again of the power of connecting our learning to the passion and caring already present in students.

Assignments for Greater Meaning

Assignments often took students beyond the classroom doors. Several larger assignments focused on practical application of textbook material. These often included focused observations in early childhood programs, in-depth interviews, development of curriculum ideas, or a process of gathering information from the community. Shorter assignments made use of personal reflections of concepts discussed in class. My overall goal was for the women to use their initiative and to trust their instincts as they gathered ideas. Projects requiring participation in the community helped break the isolation commonly felt by women in poverty. As teachers, part of their function with parents will be as liaison with community resources. One of the major projects for the Head Start class was to compile a community resource notebook.

Yolanda was not happy with this assignment. Growing up in an immigrant family, she did not trust community agencies and tried to manage on her own as a single parent. She reluctantly did the assignment, visiting eight agencies. To her surprise, everyone she interviewed was friendly and helpful. In addition to being proud of her new resource book, Yolanda began feeling more confident about making use of these resources. Unknown to her, this assignment would soon play an important role in her life.

Yolanda's oldest son was 11 and starting to get into trouble. One day he was caught trying to shoplift an item at a local store. Frightened by this new development, she remembered her own resource book. She called a police officer she had interviewed and told him she was worried about her son. She made arrangements to bring her son to meet with him. The police officer described to the child in frightening detail what it would be like if he were placed in jail. He gave Yolanda's son a chance to see what it felt like to be handcuffed, and he described a prison cell. He then asked her son what kinds of things he would like to do in his life, outside of jail. Yolanda excitedly described in class the dramatic impact this experience had on her son. Most important,

Yolanda was discovering a new sense of power in connecting to the larger community.

Other projects focused on enhancing students' self-expression, research, and academic skills. They typically included investigation of a topic of interest, a five-minute talk to the class, written and oral assignments on children's literature, and preparation of classroom materials, such as persona dolls of varying ethnicities.

Shorter assignments required observations and personal reflections. These provided an opportunity for self-reflection and for applying concepts in the students' homes and neighborhoods. Writings focused on observations of their patterns of communication, examination of their own life histories, critical analyses of media messages, observations of children, and examples of ways in which bias influenced their own lives.

Reading assignments were selective, requiring only the portions of chapters that addressed the topic most directly. I was finding that more reading did not necessarily enhance learning. In fact, it often turned student retention into shallow memorization, overwhelming the capacity to thoughtfully reflect upon ideas. Articles from current journals in the field and the students' self-selection of relevant material supplemented the readings.

Written feedback provided an opportunity for me to engage in an ongoing dialogue with each student. My written responses were extensive and helped to give a clearer and more constructive assessment. I included both positive comments and needed improvements. In this way, I could regularly track the progress of individual students. Continued assessment was essential even in the case of long-term assignments.

Students kept a portfolio of their work. The theme of societal prejudice ran like a connecting thread. This prejudice is also the reality underlying the suffering and oppression for the women of color living in poverty who were interviewed in this book. We need to look at some unexamined ways the effects of prejudice apply to our work as college instructors. In so doing we are defining our profession as an avenue to a more humane world.

Addressing Issues of Bias
The field of early childhood education has been at the forefront in exploring the challenges of raising children in our highly diverse society. The groundbreaking work of the antibias curriculum brought out the issues of bias with young children. Louise Derman-Sparks and the ABC Task Force (1989)[8] published an antibias curriculum to address "the spoken and unspoken messages regarding racism, sexism and handicappism which influence the developing child" (p. ix). The Task Force discovered that the prejudices existing in our society were already becoming part of our children's identity during the preschool years, and teachers needed to examine this reality as part of their curriculum. Janet Gonzalez-Mena (2001)[9] expanded upon this idea to include an antibias approach for working in partnership with parents and persevering in a better understanding of cultural information, adult relations, and possible conflicts with child-rearing practices.

Carter and Curtis (1994)[10] discovered in their workshops that teachers in our early childhood programs needed to face their own issues of bias. They found that teachers cannot simply be told to use the antibias curriculum with the children. They had to recognize their own biases and understand the need for this type of curriculum.

Including antibias work in my teacher preparation classes brought a new level of meaning and vitality to all our learning. In a self-reflection exercise, I asked the students to describe a personal experience in which they had been stereotyped and how this experience affected them. After a period of reflection and paired-sharing, some of the students spoke to the class about their experiences.

Rocio remembered the day her mother took her on a special shopping trip for her birthday present. She described how they went to a "nice mall in a White area." Rocio noticed people staring at them. When they went into a store, the salesperson followed them from a distance. Rocio finally found an item to buy, but nobody would help them. Each person walked away and pretended to be busy. Mother and daughter finally left. Everyone listened with silent recognition. I asked Rocio why she thought they were treated that way. She responded, "Because we are Mexican." I asked how it felt. Standing there with tears in her eyes, she recalled, "Like we're not okay. We didn't fit in, and they didn't want us there."

Bias characteristically targets our nontraditional students from ethnic minorities. To exclude this reality from our classes is similar to the proverbial elephant that people pretend not to see in their own living room. Following our class discussion of how they have been affected by stereotyping and bias, we continued with another self-reflection exercise, this time on their own prejudices. These produced a large array of labels, beliefs about different groups, and experiences of treating others with intolerance. The discussion spilled into the many ways bias can affect the children and parents they will be working with as teachers. The atmosphere in the classroom began shifting from tension to increasing understanding of the ways everyone in our society is affected by prejudice.

Just as teachers of young children must recognize their own biases, college instructors must also develop this inner awareness. As I found out with my first class of immigrant women, we need to address our own unexamined assumptions and prejudices. The inclusive nature of community colleges means that most instructors will be working with high levels of student diversity. And the complexity of these issues is increasing with the changing nature of our world. Large-scale immigration is one of the most important social developments of our time. Currently, there are more than 130 million migrants worldwide and a total foreign-born population of nearly 30 million people in the United States alone. Children of immigrants make up 20% of all youth in the United States. Adding to the growing numbers is the changing pattern of our immigrant populations. Ethnicity has shifted from European immigrants to primarily Latin and Asian populations, and the number of immigrants entering the United States has increased by 20 million since 1965 (Suarez-Orozco and Suarez Orozco, 2001).[11] We are rapidly connecting with greater intimacy to differing cultures, races, lifestyles, and religions.

On a daily basis we grapple with students confronting problems not of their making. Through journal writing I was able to recognize the ways that unconscious beliefs were affecting my interactions with students. I found it helpful to share this introspection with a trusted friend or supportive colleagues. We have chosen work that requires us to face some of the most profound, disturbing, and unresolved issues in our modern society. And these are the difficulties few of us are ready for as we greet our new students.

Our Story

As college instructors in early childhood education, we are well prepared for our work on many levels. We have a good academic background, and many of us have been active practitioners with children, parents, and families. We bring an understanding of the academics of the field we are teaching. Yet, we have been educated within the very system that needs changing if it is to reach our nontraditional students who are particularly at risk. Our conception of teacher preparation has been one of passing on a particular body of knowledge as the only truth. The growing diversity of our population is challenging this perception and asking us to recognize truth as it fits the situation (Lubeck, 1996). [12]

My work with women in poverty not only pushed me into new ways of teaching. But it also brought me face-to-face with new levels of personal discomfort. Like my students, I was facing uncertainty and risk as I let go of known answers and searched for new ones. Yet, once I allowed students to become the curriculum, even when that meant hearing stories that left me feeling emotionally raw and confused, I could never go back to safer curriculum plans.

In addition to journal writing, I began reading books and articles by instructors exploring new approaches to teaching. Their writings often began appearing in my journal as I reflected upon how I could use new ideas to enhance my teaching. Benard (1993)[13] found that there is virtual disregard for the fact that teachers need a nurturing climate and support system. In her research on fostering resilience in students, she found that it is ultimately an "inside-out" process that depends on educators taking care of themselves.

As educators, we must develop the traits we want to bring to our students. I wanted my students to explore and understand their personal experiences in order to become effective teachers of children. The same principles applied to me. I couldn't work clearly with these experiences and emotions in the classroom without doing my own inner work. As Jersild (1955)[14] wrote, "teacher's understanding of others can be only as deep as the wisdom she possesses when she looks inward upon herself. The more genuinely she looks inward, seeks to face her own problems the more able she is to realize her kinship with others" (p. 83).

Just as our classrooms can become safe places for inner reflection and growth within our common purpose of caring for children, colleges can begin to develop their own supportive forums for instructors. According to bell hooks (1994),[15] in order to grow as instructors, we have to learn how to appreciate difficulty in our own stages of intellectual development. Conversations with other faculty members who were searching for new approaches to teaching were stimulating and affirming. I was often struck by how imaginative a neighboring instructor had been in finding new ways to support students. These were all reminders that, like our students, we were writing our own new story as educators.

Charting New Territory
Early childhood education is a field that sits at the cutting edge of historical forces changing our population, family patterns, and styles of living. Meeting the needs of children and parents requires continual walking through new terrain. When I began to confer with colleagues, I experienced great relief in discovering that I did not have to walk this path alone. My own students continued to be a valuable resource as well. Together, we could expand beyond the limitations of a "banking approach," in which I needed to provide all the answers.

In my readings by educators exploring a feminine perspective in their teaching practices, I discovered possibilities for a broader range of approaches to instruction. In particular, women who used narrative and stories for bringing the voice of silenced students into our classrooms gave me encouragement and new ideas. Their courage and willingness to explore innovative ways of teaching provided reassurance as I began creating my own fragile new structures.

The volatile times we live in hold a clear message: we must find ways of understanding and connecting with highly diverse populations of people everywhere. The boundaries of our field are extending beyond national borders as the importance of working with young children is recognized throughout the world. The stakes are high. Our field can hold the key to facing and resolving the unprecedented changes that surround us. The concluding chapter examines the critical and larger implications of this new journey.

NOTES

1   In 1985, GAIN (Greater Avenues for Independence) was established in California to facilitate job training, employment, and support for welfare recipients. These functions have been largely shifted to CalWORKs as part of welfare reform.

2   Grumet, Madeleine R. *Bitter Milk: Women and Teaching.* Amherst, MA: University of Massachusetts Press, 1988.

3   Jones, Elizabeth. Introduction to *Growing Teachers: Partnerships in Staff Development,* edited by Elizabeth Jones. Washington, DC: NAEYC, 1993.

4   Noddings, Nel. *Caring: A Feminine Approach to Ethics and Moral Education.* Berkeley, CA. University of California Press, 1984.

5   Carter, Margie, and Deb Curtis. *Training Teachers: A Harvest of Theory and Practice.* St. Paul, MN: Redleaf Press, 1994. This book gives a philosophical basis and practical strategies for staff development that go beyond a "banking method" of learning.

6   hooks, bell. *Teaching to Transgress: Education as the Practice of Freedom.* New York: Routledge, 1994. This book looks at the possibility of our classes becoming exciting places that promote freedom of thought rather than reinforcing dominant ideas.

7   Jersild, Arthur T. *When Teachers Face Themselves.* New York: Teachers College Press, 1955.

8   Derman-Sparks, Louise, and the ABC Task Force. *Antibias Curriculum: Tools for Empowering Young Children.* Washington, DC: NAEYC, 1989. Practical ideas are given that facilitate teachers to address issues of bias among children.

9   Gonzalez-Mena, Janet. *Multicultural Issues in Child Care.* Mountain View, CA: Mayfield Publishing Co., 2001. This book shows how caregivers can honor diversity in their work with families in childcare programs.

10 Carter, Margie, and Deb Curtis. *Training Teachers: A Harvest of Theory and Practice.* St. Paul, MN: Redleaf Press, 1994.

11 Suarez-Orozco, Carola, and Marcelo M. Suarez-Orozco. *Children of Immigration.* Cambridge, MA: Harvard University Press, 2001.

12 Lubeck, Sally. "Deconstructing Child Development Knowledge and Teacher Preparation." *Early Childhood Research Quarterly*, 11 (1996): 147-67.

13 Benard, Bonnie. "Fostering Resiliency in Kids." *Educational Leadership* 51 no. 3 (1993): 44–48.

14 Jersild, Arthur T. *When Teachers Face Themselves.* New York: Teachers College Press, 1955.

15 hooks, bell. *Teaching to Transgress: Education as the Practice of Freedom.* New York: Routledge, 1994.

Chapter 8

Walking the Open Road

Sunlight streamed through the windows onto our row of potted plants. Bright pictures and soft carpeting made a comfortable setting for the fifteen small chairs. The children sat in a semicircle for story time. But today was different. They were looking at me with wide, anxious eyes. This was our last day together, and I saw the fear on their faces. What could I say that would give them comfort and courage? I turned to the healing power of story and a brave little fish called Swimmy (Lionni, 1963).[1] Slowly and with great tenderness, I began reading.

Every child was mesmerized by the little fish who had just lost everything. A big fish had swallowed the others, leaving Swimmy frightened, lost, and alone. He swam away, looking around at the strange new world he just entered. I didn't want to rush through this part of the book. I stopped reading and looked into each face: "It can feel scary and sad to leave everybody and go someplace new, can't it?" They nodded, wide-eyed. At 5 years old, they understood what I was talking about. They were leaving the world they knew to join a bigger one called "kindergarten."

Swimmy begins to find his new world more and more interesting. He discovers strange and wondrous things he had never seen before. He grows strong and adventurous but never forgets the big fish that swallowed his family. When he finally meets another school of fish, he teaches them how to take care of themselves while enjoying the beauty of their lives. As I closed the book, Mary Beth happily announced, "I know how to take care of myself, too. I'm going to a big school, and I'm just scared a little. I can tie my own shoes and feed Bushy the cat." We were ready to begin our next conversation.

Even at 5 years old, the children seemed to know that life holds a mysterious combination of forces. I wanted to remind them that their mixed feelings were okay. And they could use all their new experiences to learn and grow strong. On that day, Swimmy the fish did my work for me. Like Swimmy, our children will need to find their way in an unknown and unpredictable world.

Looking into the Mirror
The last century has shown us the great dangers implicit in many of our previous assumptions about world problems. Our increasing interconnectedness will no longer allow the illusion of safety through separation. We are learning that no country or group can be shielded from the persecutions that others face. We can no longer dismiss those with differing beliefs, experiences, and views without endangering our own lives. Our carefully planned systems of attack and defense can now be used against us. Along with our borders, the scientifically calculated answers we have developed are rapidly disintegrating.

As the twenty-first century began, America was faced with a crisis that pitted us in a desperate struggle for new answers. The unfolding events of September 11, 2001, left us speechless and grieving. Strangely lacking were words to voice the depth of our sorrow and loss. We felt helpless as we tried to grapple with our country's massive sorrow.

An article in the *Los Angeles Times* during this horrific week discussed the inadequacy of our language to express wrenching emotions amid chaos and uncertainty. The poet and journalist Ruben Martinez believes we were trying to use a language for something we don't have language for. Our country has shielded itself from tragedy and has a language of optimism. Yet, beneath this optimism, others see a fear of pain and grief. Educator bell hooks remarks that we have a disconnected language based on emotional distance. "As a nation, we don't want to hear the language of suffering. We replace it with vengeance....In this language of war, we can't allow this face where pain can be felt and public grief" (George, Tawa, Dimassa, 17 September 2001, sec. E1, p. 13).[2]

America is a country built on the ideals and success of modern science. Our language reflects both the strengths and limitations of these beliefs. Our words are rich in objective and technical terms and deeply oriented toward solving problems and controlling outcomes. In the aftermath of September 11, the paradigm of scientific thought became inadequate. We instinctively began searching for a way to go beyond the emotional distance of a scientific language. Our pain brought us to the convoluted yet profoundly inspiring stories of real people.

Only the living stories of individuals facing difficult and life-threatening choices during this time could capture the true nature of the extraordinary drama taking place. Their stories brought together a strange mixture of pain, courage, and inner strength as they made bold choices with no guaranteed outcome. They captured the hidden power and mystery of human nature that are lost in the abstract and disconnected language of our modern objective thought and vocabulary.

Early childhood education must pay close attention to the limitations in our current educational theory. We have an opportunity to learn important lessons from the gaping void that became apparent in the face of shocking pain. Our work with young children places us at the leading edge of future developments. These children will not only need to adapt to new conditions, but also will be the ones responsible for forming its direction. The tragedy of September 11 was a sudden glimpse into a future we were not prepared to understand. More than ever, we need a wide-ranging and inclusive approach to education.

The Problematic Nature of Living
Amid the chaos of unforeseen local and world events, one message is becoming apparent. We do not live in a predictable world that can be controlled, packaged, and made safe. Early childhood programs will

need teachers to help children and families to function effectively in the face of unexpected events, unfamiliar people and cultures, rapid change, and differing forms of truth. Yet, our knowledge base is filled with restraints. We need to find the words. We need to discover a vocabulary that gives voice to the many dimensions of our lives, from sorrow and joy to scientific data. The repercussions of these constraints are becoming evident throughout our field.

Our teacher preparation programs have not been able to resolve the frustrating dilemma of educating the growing numbers of nontraditional students entering early childhood education. This condition is further complicated by the difficulties we are facing in serving the complex needs of an increasingly diverse population of children and families. Adding to our challenges are the rapidly changing lifestyles and living conditions of modern families.

Our human zeal for finding answers to the complex problems of living can lead to oversimplifying reality, diminishing our capacity for true growth and healing. Lillian Katz (1996),[3] an early childhood educator, questions the messages contained within developmental theory, which is based on predicting change over time. She is concerned that we are making implicit and explicit assumptions about the relationships between experiences provided for young children and the long-term effects of those experiences.

These oversimplified assumptions hold a clear message for children and adults living in the difficult conditions of poverty, problematic families, or ethnic and racial oppression. What do our theories say to a single mother in poverty working to support three children? What if she cannot provide quality time, enrichment activities, a safe neighborhood, and consistent care and attention for her children? Our theoretical assumptions imply that children in such circumstances are destined to become poorly functioning adults. Current theory needs to pay greater attention to the stories of human courage and stunning success in spite of and perhaps because of difficulties endured, spiritual values, unpredictable events, and other nonmeasurable dimensions of life.

Beneath our focus on cause/effect predictions and generalized rules for healthy development, we are communicating a fearful need to control life. This belief has moved us away from a sense of wholeness and the self-trust that comes from embracing the problematic, painful, and unexpected dimensions of real life. Very simply, we cannot shield our children from life itself, and perhaps realistic acceptance of problems is the most lasting protection.

Parents often manifest implicit fears in their belief that they must provide perfect environments and lives for their children in order to ensure healthy development. A recent article, "A Generation Un-scathed" (Straight, 12 August 2001),[4] discusses parents' fearful obsession over risks of children getting hurt, physically or emotionally. The author discusses new rules set up at schools: swings being removed, dodge ball no longer allowed, children never allowed out of our sight. She wonders "if there are risks to the brain, the psyche, the muscles, when all risks are averted. What are we teaching children who can't ride bikes and climb trees and play baseball in a vacant lot, who can't slide and fall on the sand in school, or play dodge ball, who can't learn to settle their own fights and negotiate the social territory of childhood and adolescence?" (Magazine, p. 13)

Maslow (1968)[5] has expressed his concern about the dangers that lie beneath our easy distinction between sickness and health. He believes that growth and self-fulfillment are not possible without pain and grief and sorrow and turmoil. He finds people who have problems such as struggle, conflict, guilt, anxiety, depression, frustration, and shame are considered sick and need to be cured as soon as possible. Yet, all of these symptoms are also found in healthy people. Although adjustment and stabilization are considered good because they reduce our pain, they also impede independence and resourcefulness.

Our nontraditional students may hold critically important gifts needed by our field, and perhaps by our world, at this time. Their hidden gifts are not ones of comfort and security. Like any misfit or stranger, they are bringing us face-to-face with our limitations. They are telling us that our educational structures are running the risk of becoming exclusive and classist. They are a reminder of Regina's warning,

> *I don't believe in people like judging other people. You can't tell anything. Even if a person says something. Unless you know what they've been through, you don't actually know them.*

Our job in education is to bring students closer to the many types of people, cultures, and families they will be serving as teachers. It is to challenge and provoke people to climb beyond the confines of their known world. Our classrooms need to become places where we learn to listen and share a great variety of stories that present differing perspectives and reflect the complex nature of real lives. Living stories are messy. There are no clear villains or predictable outcomes. They can teach us a deeper sense of possibilities for health and living.

As educators, we must allow ourselves the discomfort that goes with reflecting upon life beyond the framework of our known theories. We need to listen to the infinite ways that people face life and discover themselves in the process of living. Our scientific insights will not disappear as a result of being challenged by differing perspectives. They will become expanded, refined, and more complex. They will include everyone's voice.

Walking the Open Road

The women in this book have walked the road of shocking devastation. They have watched all their hopes turn against them. They have experienced their fragile world disintegrate without a safety net to catch their fall. Many women in similar situations succumbed to the devastation wreaked on them. Overwhelmed with pain, responsibilities, and little or no personal support, they gave up hope of finding a way out. Others, like Swimmy, mysteriously discovered a new inner strength that eventually brought them into our classrooms. And like Swimmy, they bring with them much valuable awareness from their suffering. They have not forgotten their painful experiences. These very struggles became a source of passionate desire to help others. They have walked the open road that holds no clear answers while the world they knew slipped away.

The women's free-form narratives take us into a world filled with the powerful dynamics of real-life experience. This is a world that includes the mysteries of inner awareness, unpredictable outcomes, pain and suffering, and the unfolding of nonlinear patterns of growth. Their stories take us beyond the constraints of a scientific cause/effect perspective of life that has little role for pain, except as a predictor for flawed development. Dimitria shares the value of telling her story:

> It allows me to go back and see where I was and where I'm at today. It keeps me focused. And what a difference! You know? And I am not ashamed of what I have been through. It is a hurting factor to be human today. After all that and I could have been here! But you know it is a learning process. And I

just feel like patting myself and saying, "Well, I've been through a learning experience. And that road I'll never have to go down again."

Our children will need teachers who can help them and their families develop the kind of strength that comes from fully embracing life. We need to find pathways to real wholeness. This can only take place as we begin seeing the value of the struggles we are all facing, and models for health that can blossom under many different circumstances, from the idyllic country home to the inner-city apartment to the shelter for the homeless.

The dramatically changing times that we are living in keep showing us the inadequacy of perfect ideals to guide our lives. Our society needs to be shown new possibilities for discovering strength and well-being. The women's stories can help take us there. Their narratives are healing because they are free from judgments. They bring people back to the power of their true lives and who they can become. They tell highly complex stories in both content and outcome. The women view their lives through multiple perspectives in a search for wisdom and understanding. In challenging our limited beliefs, their stories may be offering a much-needed new perspective of human development.

Our Continuing Legacy

The women's stories in this book tell more than the complexity of human development. They are breaking the silence of oppression. They are giving voice to women all over the world who, amid unconscionable conditions of poverty, violence, hunger, and loneliness, have not given up. They represent the invisible women in society who are disdained or ignored while attempting to raise children, maintain jobs, take buses, shop, clean, and cook. Most important, their stories tell of a dream. It is a dream we must pay careful attention to in our field. It is the dream that brings them into our programs. Often ill-prepared for our academic world, they sit in our classes as silent misfits. Yet, their vision of using their lives to help children and families is intrinsic to the continuing legacy of early childhood education.

For centuries, educators from Plato and Froebel to Piaget and Freire have seen our work as holding the promise of a more peaceful world. This vision comes out of our dedication to social justice through respecting and honoring each person's life as a gift to humanity. In particular, early childhood educators know the importance of recognizing and nurturing the unfolding unique gifts each child brings into our world.

During the horrifying political developments of the 1930s, Maria Montessori (1949)[6] presented a series of lectures to various governments and universities pleading for a shift in our direction from war to peace. In each lecture, she described work with young children as the vehicle for transforming our world. Her warnings about the direction of world events and the unseen gaps in humanity's development are equally relevant today:

> *A new world for a new man—this is our most urgent need....The crisis we are experiencing is not the sort of upheaval that marks the passage from one historical period to another. It can be compared only to one of those biological or geological epochs in which new, higher, more perfect forms of life appeared, as totally new conditions of existence on earth came about (p. 23).*

> *Who will sound the trumpet awakening him? Man today lies slumbering on the surface of the earth, which is about to swallow him up. What will he do? ...Our principal concern must be to educate humanity—the human beings of all nations—in order to guide it toward seeking common goals. We must turn back and make the child our principal concern (pp. 26, 31).*

Early childhood education is part of a growing awareness of the importance that learning holds for our lives. It has expanded into every country around the world. At no time in history has our potential impact been greater. And at no time were the risks higher for humankind than they are today. The opportunity for preparing teachers on a global basis brings with it the responsibility of learning to work with diverse populations in a respectful and meaningful way.

We must begin with our own transformation as we expand beyond a Euro-American, masculine, and scientifically designed structure for perceiving human development. New emphasis must be placed on teaching practices that are inclusive of all types of students. As in any type of deep-seated change, it will require a willingness to be uncomfortable and disoriented as we find our way.

Listening to the women's stories reveals our common humanity. Even from the perspective of my comparatively comfortable life, there were no emotions I could not relate to. I have felt loneliness, rejection, inadequacy as a parent, and fear of living in a world that may not care if I needed help. I have loved, made mistakes, learned about life, taken risks, and became committed to working toward a better world. I also knew that I grew and became a stronger, more compassionate person as a result of difficulties in my own life.

Yet, their stories present an ominous warning. They illuminate the dangers present in our unquestioned definitions of the way life is and who deserves to be called a healthy person. Our unseen limitations and distortions may be costing us more than we care to know. They may be costing us the compassion and vision needed to truly educate our students and bring us closer to a world that will not destroy itself.

It may be that until we can embrace all parts of being human, we will continue to pretend that we are different from those who are suffering. Or at best, pity them and try to fix them. We need to teach about a world in which we are all learning and struggling together to make life work. Only then can we use our knowledge to benefit everybody and allow our field to grow from all those participating. The women's gift was that of telling the truth. Our gift, in return, can be to take our field to a new level of wisdom.

NOTES

1   Lionni, Leo. *Swimmy.* New York: Pantheon Books, 1963.

2   George, Lynell, Renee Tawa, and Cara Mia Dimassa, "Groping for Words," *Los Angeles Times,* 17 September 2001, sec. E1, p. 13.

3   Katz, Lillian G. "Child Development Knowledge and Teacher Preparation: Confronting Assumptions." *Early Childhood Research Quarterly* 11 (1996): 137–46.

4   Straight, R. "A Generation Unscathed," *Los Angeles Times*, 12 August 2001, Magazine, p. 13.

5   Maslow, Abraham. *Toward a Psychology of Being.* New York: Van Nostrand Reinhold Company Inc., 1968.

6   Montessori, Maria. *Education and Peace.* Chicago: Henry Regnery Company, 1949. This book is composed of talks presented by Montessori during the 1930s which give warning and ask penetrating philosophical questions regarding current political directions. They are a plea to move toward a lasting peace through the education of our children.

Bibliography

Belenky, Mary F., Blythe M. Clinchy, Nancy R. Goldberger, and Jill M. Tarule. *Women's Ways of Knowing: The Development of Self, Voice, and Mind.* New York: Basic Books, 1986.

Belle, Deborah. "Poverty and Women's Mental Health." *American Psychologist* 45, no. 3 (1990): 385–89.

Benard, Bonnie. "Fostering Resiliency in Kids." *Educational Leadership* 51, no. 3 (1993): 44–48.

Bloom, Paula J. *Avoiding Burnout: Strategies for Managing Time, Space, and People in Early Childhood Education.* Lake Forest, IL: New Horizons, 1982.

Borden, William. "Narrative Perspectives in Psychosocial Intervention Following Adverse Life Events." *Social Work* 37, no. 2 (1992): 135–41.

Carter, Margie, and Deb Curtis. *Training Teachers: A Harvest of Theory and Practice.* St. Paul, MN: Redleaf Press, 1994.

Children's Defense Fund. *Poverty Matters: The Cost of Child Poverty in America.* Washington, DC: Children's Defense Fund, 1998.

———. *The State of America's Children.* Washington, DC: Children's Defense Fund, 2000.

Cost, Quality and Child Outcomes Study Team. *Cost, Quality, and Child Outcomes in Child Care Centers*. Denver, CO: University of Colorado, 1995.

Daloz, Laurent, A. P., Cheryl H. Keen, James P. Keen, and Sharon D. Parks. *Common Fire: Leading Lives of Commitment in a Complex World*. Boston, MA: Beacon Press, 1996.

Delpit, Lisa. *Other People's Children: Cultural Conflict in the Classroom*. New York: The New Press, 1995.

Derman-Sparks, Louise, and the ABC Task Force. *Anti-bias Curriculum: Tools for Empowering Young Children*. Washington, DC: NAEYC, 1989.

Espin, Olivia M. *Latina Realities: Essays on Healing, Migration, and Sexuality*. Boulder, CO: Westview Press, 1997.

Freire, Paulo. *Pedagogy of the Oppressed*. New York: The Continuum Publishing Co., 1997.

George, Lynell, Renee Tawa, and Cara Mia Dimassa. "Groping for Words." *Los Angeles Times*, 17 September 2001, E1.

Gilligan, Carol. *In a Different Voice*. Cambridge, MA: Harvard University Press, 1982.

Gonzalez-Mena, Janet. *Multicultural Issues in Child Care*. Mountain View, CA: Mayfield Publishing Co., 2001.

Greene, B. "African American Women." In *Women of Color: Integrating Ethnic and Gender Identities in Psychotherapy*, edited by L. Comas-Diaz and B. Greene, 10–29. New York: The Guilford Press, 1994.

Grumet, Madeleine R. *Bitter Milk: Women and Teaching*. Amherst, MA: University of Massachusetts Press, 1988.

Harrison, Algea O., Melvin N. Wilson, Charles J. Pine, Samuel Q. Chan, and Raymond Buriel. "Family Ecologies of Ethnic Minority Children." *Child Development* 61, no. 2 (1990) 348–362.

Hendrick, Joanne. *The Whole Child*, 7th ed. Englewood Cliffs, NJ: Prentice Hall, Inc., 1996.

hooks, bell. *Teaching to Transgress: Education as the Practice of Freedom*. New York: Routledge, 1994.

Jersild, Arthur T. *When Teachers Face Themselves*. New York: Teachers College Press,   1955.

Jones, Elizabeth. "Constructing Professional Knowledge by Telling Our Stories." In *The Early Childhood Career Lattice: Perspective on Professional Development,* edited by J. Johnson and J. McCracken. Washington, DC: NAEYC, 1994.

———. Introduction to *Growing Teachers: Partnerships in Staff Development,* edited by Elizabeth Jones. Washington, DC: NAEYC, 1993.

———. *Teaching Adults: An Active Learning Approach.* Washington, DC: NAEYC, 1986.

Kaplin, Paul S. *A Child's Odyssey: Child and Adolescent Development,* 3rd. Belmont, CA: Wadsworth/Thomson Learning, 2000.

Katz, Lillian G. "Child Development Knowledge and Teacher Preparation: Confronting Assumptions." *Early Childhood Research Quarterly* 11 (1996): 137–46.

Kaufman, Gershen. *Shame: The Power of Caring.* Cambridge, MA: Schenkman Publishing Co. Inc., 1980.

Lifton, Robert J. *Human Resilience in an Age of Fragmentation.* New York: Basic Books, 1993.

Lionni, Leo. *Swimmy.* New York: Pantheon Books, 1963.

Lubeck, Sally. "Deconstructing child development knowledge and teacher preparation." *Early Childhood Research Quarterly* 11 (1996): 147–67.

Maslow, Abraham. *Toward a Psychology of Being.* New York: Van Nostrand Reinhold Company Inc., 1968.

McAdoo, H. "African-American Families: Strengths and Realities." In *Resiliency in African American Families,* edited by H. McCubbin, E. Thompson, A. Thompson, and J. Futrell, 17–30. Thousand Oaks, CA: Sage Publications, Inc., 1998.

Montessori, Maria. *Education and Peace.* Chicago: Henry Regnery Company, 1949.

National Center for Education Statistics. *First Generation Students: Undergraduates Whose Parents Never Enrolled in Postsecondary Education.* NCES 1–41. Washington, DC, 1998.

Noddings, Nel. *Caring: A Feminine Approach to Ethics and Moral Education.* Berkeley, CA. University of California Press, 1984.

———. "Stories in Dialogue: Caring and Interpersonal Reasoning." In *Stories Lives Tell: Narrative and Dialogue in Education* edited by

Carol Witherell and Nel Noddings, 157–70. New York: Teachers College Press, 1991.

Noddings, Nel, and Paul J. Shore. *Awakening the Inner Eye: Intuition in Education*. New York: Teachers College Press, 1984.

Pagano, Jo Anne. *Exiles and Communities: Teaching in the Patriarchal Wilderness*. Albany, NY: State University of New York Press, 1990.

Palmer, Parker J. *To Know as We Are Known*. New York: Harper Collins Publishers, 1993.

Polakow, Valerie. *Lives on the Edge: Single Mothers and Their Children in the Other America*. Chicago: The University of Chicago Press, 1993.

Shabatay, Virginia. "The Stranger's Story: Who Calls and Who Answers?" In *Stories Lives Tell: Narrative and Dialogue in Education*, edited by Carol Witherell and Nel Noddings, 136–52. New York: Teachers College Press, 1991.

Sidel, Ruth. "The Enemy Within: A Commentary on the Demonization of Difference." *American Journal of Orthopsychiatry*, 66, no. 4 (1996): 490–95.

Straight, Susan. "A Generation Unscathed." *Los Angeles Times*, 12 September 2001, Magazine E 13.

Suarez-Orozco, Carola, and Marcelo M. Suarez-Orozco. *Children of Immigration*. Cambridge, MA: Harvard University Press, 2001.

Tappan, Mark B., and Lyn Mikel Brown. "Stories Told and Lessons Learned: Toward a Narrative Approach to Moral Development and Moral Education." In *Stories Lives Tell: Narrative and Dialogue in Education* edited by Carol Witherell and Nel Noddings. New York: Teachers College Press, 1991.

Witherell Carol, and Nel Noddings. Prologue to *Stories Lives Tell: Narrative and Dialogue in Education*, edited by Carol Witherell and Nel Noddings, 1–12. New York: Teachers College Press, 1991.

Index

Note: Topics that appear in the context of an individual's story are so indicated by the subheading "in personal narrative."

RETHINKING CHILDHOOD

GAILE S. CANNELLA, *General Editor*

Researchers in a range of fields have acknowledged that childhood is a construct emerging from modernist perspectives that have not always benefited those who are younger. The purpose of the Rethinking Childhood Series is to provide a critical location for scholarship that challenges the universalization of childhood and introduces new, reconceptualized, and critical spaces from which opportunities and possibilities are generated for children. Diverse histories and cultures are considered of major importance as well as issues of critical social justice.

We are particularly interested in manuscripts that provide insight into the contemporary neoliberal conditions experienced by those who are labeled "children" as well as authored and edited volumes that illustrate life and educational experiences that challenge present conditions. Rethinking childhood work related to critical education and care, childhood public policy, family and community voices, and critical social activism is encouraged.

For more information about this series or for submission of manuscripts, please contact:

Gaile S. Cannella
Gaile.Cannella@unt.edu

To order other books in this series, please contact our Customer Service Department at:

(800) 770-LANG (within the U.S.)
(212) 647-7706 (outside the U.S.)
(212) 647-7707 FAX

Or browse online by series at:
www.peterlang.com